COLOMBIA REAL ESTATE

SECRETS

The Ultimate Guide to Buying and Investing in Properties from abroad, for Those Who Don't Know Where to Start, are Seasoned Investors, or Want to Relocate without Hassles

Mauricio Jaimes

Copyright

This book is intended as an informative tool for your guidance only. The author has made every effort while preparing the material contained within the book to ensure its accuracy and reliability. However, nothing in this book constitutes financial, tax or any other such professional advice and the author recommend that the reader seeks independent financial advice or other professional advice, where necessary, regarding their financial status, particular issues and risks associated with property investing and how they put into practice some of the tools within this book.

Disclaimer

Whilst every effort has been made to ensure the accuracy of the information contained in this book, it is a condition of sale that the author shall in no event be held liable for any loss directly or indirectly arising from any use of the material contained within the book. It is also a condition of sale that the author will accept no liability for any inaccuracies, errors or omissions within the book

TABLE OF CONTENTS

INTRODUCTION

Are you planning to buy or invest in Colombian real estate?

Do you have a Colombian wife or husband who is encouraging you to invest in Colombian real estate? Are you relocating to Colombia because of your work? Do you already have ties to this beautiful country?

If your answer is yes to any of these questions, you have probably considered buying Colombian properties.

Don't know where to start?

Well, here is what you've been searching for. This is a complete guide on **How to buy Colombian real estate**.

There is not enough information in **English** about Colombia real estate. So, I decided to make this guide for the foreigner who has found a place in Colombia to live, rent, retire or invest and who wants some help with one of the biggest decisions a newcomer can make: **Buying a home**. If this guide also convinces at least one foreign person to become a Colombian national, that would be awesome!!

I love this country and I would love for people all over the world to be able to discover the great things Colombia has to offer and the wonderful place it is to live.

I want to share with you my more than **twenty-five years of experience** in the Colombian **construction and real estate** industry and provide you with the **information** containing everything you need to know to make the most of your investment.

Most Colombian real estate websites assume you already are a real estate expert and that you know almost everything, frequently showing you only "gringo listings". I understand that you may not be familiar with Colombia. You may have many questions about how the laws in Colombia differ from those of your home country. Eventually you may find yourself asking, "Why hasn't anybody told me these things before?"

This guide offers you:

- The most accurate information about **how the process of buying** real estate in Colombia works.

- A step-by-step **guide** to the entire process. Information about **how to proceed when paying for your property.**

- Recommendations for before you buy. Simple rules to follow if you're thinking of becoming a **property investor** in Colombia.

- Real estate characteristics of the most popular cities in Colombia, including **Bogota, Cartagena, Medellin, Cali, and Bucaramanga.**

- **Legal and tax** related issues regarding foreign investment in Colombia.

- All related **laws regarding real estate** in Colombia.

Among much more important information.

I hope you can find all the **answers to your questions** in this book, but if you don't, you can visit my website www.buycolombiarealty.com and use the contact form and I'll find out who has the answer!

Never forget the three most important rules that apply in the modern online world that are also beginning to change the world of buying real estate abroad…

… Information, Information, Information!

Although, traditional ones are also important too: **Location, Location and Location!**

Here you will find a good mix of these six rules. At the end you will feel **confident**, **safe** and most importantly, **happy** and ready to enjoy your **property in Colombia**.

This guide is updated with your feedback. Please feel free to e-mail me your comments about anything you think will improve the quality and quantity of the information.

Let's get to business...

LIVING IN COLOMBIA: PLENTY OF REASONS TO STAY!

Have you ever thought about living in Colombia? Or is this the first time you've heard about **Colombia**?

If you are planning to move to Colombia, you may already have a reason for **loving** this country. I'm sure you do. Why don't you share it with us?

The **colorful landscapes**, the warmth of its people. The magic of the old **Cartagena**, the beautiful tiny colonial streets of **Villa de Leyva and Giron in Santander** and the taste of its unique variety of typical food. This is what Colombians miss the most when we leave Colombia.

But in case you only know about Shakira's dancing style...

Did you know that:

- We have the longest coast in the **Caribbean**

- We are the world's number one for **birds species** (1,815), **butterflies** (14,000 species) and **orchids** (3,000 families)

- World number one country in **Andean Páramo areas, the greatest natural water factories in the world.**

- We boast the **second oldest airline** in the world (*Avianca*).

- Colombia is the **longest established democracy** in South America, believe it or not!

*"If you want to know the **Caribbean**, go to Cuba or the Dominican Republic;*
*if you want to know the **Pacific Ocean**, go to Chile;*
*if you want to know the **Andean Mountains**, go to Ecuador;*
*if you want to know the **Amazon Jungle**, go to Brazil;*
*if you want to know **pre-Colombian cultures**, go to Mexico or Peru;*
*but if you want to know **all of those in just one place**, go to Colombia"*

From a Travel Agency in France. Source: Colombia es Pasión

Colombia has so much to offer to **foreigners** and visiting will forever change your previous vision of the country.

What I like the most about living in Colombia is its **geographic diversity**. When you are traveling by car it's easy to experience dramatic changes between the freezing Andean weather and the soft warm breeze of a Colonial town.

That's why we don't have traditional **seasons**. You can decide when and where to enjoy your special or favorite season.

And it's not uncommon to find similar contrasts **all over** the country. Even on the Caribbean coast you can find a snow-capped mountain right next to the sea! (La Sierra Nevada de Santa Marta).

RETIRE IN COLOMBIA

Discover all of the opportunities Colombia has to offer for a safe and productive retirement.

You might consider the idea of international living, but perhaps retiring to Colombia is the last option you'd think of. It should be acknowledged that we do have a lot of problems, but our 48 million inhabitants have to deal with the **same problems** as any other country in the world.

U.S. families have their kids fighting overseas, we have our young soldiers fighting in the jungle; insecurity in **New York** can be higher than Bogota or Medellin; drug consumption is higher in Europe than in Colombia; **South Africa, Venezuela, Jamaica and Brazil** have more gun murders than Colombia (but that is not portrayed in the media!). Kidnappings statistics are currently lower in Colombia than **Haiti and Mexico**.

9

I can keep listing all of the problems we have to deal with in this modern era. But they are all in contrast to the country's tremendous assets - a sound economic management and performance record, a democratic and constitutional tradition and educational, cultural and scientific progress.

Why not give a country a chance if it can offer you **low costs of living, quality of life, outstanding landscapes and a gentle people** all in one?

So, what's life in Colombia like? What are the people like? How's the food? How much does it cost to live? These are the kind of questions that only can be answered by visiting - even for just a couple of weeks. Don't let negative publicity spoil a **wonderful trip**.

New sensations, limitless possibilities and new and exciting beginnings may await you here.

These are some of the advantages for retirees in Colombia:

A unique location at the northwest corner of South America, two coasts (the Pacific and the Caribbean), the Andean mountains and geographic diversity.

The distance. An approximately three hour flight from Miami to Bogota, Medellin or Cali.

Climate diversity. You can choose the climate to fit your needs, or you can experience the four seasons in many different locations all around the country at any time of the year.

Cost of living. Attractive, affordable costs for high quality retirement living. A lower cost of living does not mean you have to sacrifice the quality of life you have been accustomed to in the United States, Canada or Europe. In fact, you will probably be able to live with even more luxuries than you are accustomed to, simply because the prices are so economic.

The property market offers significant bargains; a comfortable lifestyle can be enjoyed in Colombia on just a fraction of what you'd spend in many other parts of the world. Having an undervalued currency is more an advantage than a disadvantage in this case. And it will always be this way. Long-term policies are focused on strengthening export and international trade and the peso has to be devaluated in order to gain economic competitiveness.

A natural, comfortable way of living. Community complexes outside the cities in close-by natural environments are gaining in popularity in Colombia.

The simplicity of establishing your life in Colombia. Foreign investment is welcome in Colombia. The government is committed to encouraging foreign families to invest and retire in Colombia. They want to focus on attracting large numbers of retirees from the U.S and Europe. Currently, countries with coastal cities like Mexico, Costa Rica and Panama dominate this market but we know that Colombia has equal or even better advantages for retirees than some of these countries.

Right now, foreigners can purchase homes, invest, and run any business with no limitations other than those that apply to locals, and they can obtain full ownership titles.

Accessibility of commercial facilities where you can obtain your daily necessities. Large supermarket chains are already present in most Colombian cities (French retail chains like **Groupe Casino** who bought local retail chain "Exito" have stores in all major cities). They stock a wealth of local and imported groceries and general necessities.

Technology infrastructure. Good internet accessibility is due in part to the fact that Colombia maintains the third-highest telephone density network in Latin America, ahead of Brazil and Mexico.

Tropical and subtropical regions. We produce all kinds of fruits and vegetables in abundance. Fresh produce and exotic fruits are available daily in the markets around the country. You'll be surprised to taste delicious fruits you may never have heard of before.

Healthcare. An extensive modern private healthcare infrastructure exists in Colombia. You can buy health insurance for half the cost than in the US. Hospitals and clinics feature up to date medicine, trained doctors, technology, and equipment. Among many others health care institutions, Bogotá boasts the **Barraquer Clinic**, an internationally recognized eye clinic where an innovative laser technology for surgical purposes was devised; **Fundación Cardiovascular de Colombia**, one of the most advanced institutions in Latin America for heart disease treatment and **Fundación**

Oftalmológica FOSCAL, which specializes in advanced optical surgery, both of which are located in Bucaramanga, Santander department.

The famous Argentinian soccer player **Diego Maradona** chose Cartagena in 2005 to undertake the gastric-by-pass surgery that helped him lose approximately 100 pounds. In 2007 he returned to Bogota to have an aesthetic dental treatment. And it's not only famous people who consider Colombia for their medical surgeries - **regular people from around the world** come here because of the low cost and quality of results.

Ecotourism attractions. Colombia is the number one bird watching spot in the world. At the Pacific coast you can go whale watching, scuba diving or surfing. Indeed, you will find that wherever you decide to live, different outdoor activities (hiking, climbing, mountain biking, paragliding) are supported by the year-round spring weather.

The friendly nature of the Colombian people. This is our most valuable asset. People are friendly to foreigners. Even you don't speak Spanish, people in the streets will make an effort to understand you and communicate.

Take the time to explore a new place and give us the opportunity to show you our beautiful country. Discover the many opportunities for a safe and productive retirement in Colombia.

THE COLOMBIAN HOME BUYING PROCESS, A STEP BY STEP GUIDE

The home buying process in Colombia can be a pleasant experience. Just keep in mind our Buyers Tips, or if you are looking for an investment check out these Investors Tips and be prepared to take it **one step** at a time.

Let's get to business.

I have outlined the process for buying a home in these **10 steps**. This may seem like a lot of steps, but you will find it to be a logical, easy process. Each will be covered in detail throughout this guide.

1. Choose the location.

Do you have enough information about the city where you are planning to live or move? Search for as much information as you can get about the local real estate market you are planning to buy in. You will find a general overview of the best Colombian hot spots in the following chapters of this guide.

2. Choose the property.

When buying a home, begin by making a wish list of the type of property you want. Are you looking for off-plan projects? As-is, For Sale by Owner (FSBO)? Develop your knowledge of the different types of **Colombian properties** and make your choice. Utilize technology and begin your search online. Once you have a list of properties you like, prepare to take a trip to Colombia and visit those properties. Even though data driven platforms are starting to make it easier to buy properties online, it is still a good idea to see a property in-person.

3. Make an offer and negotiate the price.

In Colombia people usually overprice their properties, because buyers always undervalue other peoples' property. So, prepare to bargain. I'll show you what you need to know about estimating **home value** in Colombia.

4. Define your payment method.

Once you agree to the price, it is important to plan your **payment method** in advance. I will outline in detail the information you need to help you decide **how to pay** for your home. In my book *"How to pay for your real estate in Colombia"*, I delve deeper into this subject.

5. Sign a purchase agreement.

No matter whether you're buying or selling, once you agree to the major terms of the negotiation make sure it is confirmed on paper. We'll look at what a **sales contract** must contain to protect the buyer's rights.

6. Make the closing and sign the deed.

Many people forget what the closing phase implies in terms of legality and expenses. In this guide, I cover all of the information related to the closing and the extra money you need to reserve to pay **closing costs.**

7. Prepare to receive your property.

No matter whether you can or can't fly to Colombia to receive the keys of your property, be sure to have it covered.

8. Register the ownership of the property.

You are finally the new owner! You must now legalize it in the local government's office. Make sure to research what you should know about **recording titles**.

9. Register your property as a foreign investment.

A foreign investor can declare the entry of foreign exchange to purchase the property as a simple transfer of money or as a foreign investment in Colombia. Pros and cons are explained in chapter No. 9.

10. Enjoy your property!!

HOME BUYING TIPS

All home buying tips could be summed up in these three words: **use common sense**.

But sometimes it is not that obvious, especially if you're buying in a foreign country and you have to contend with language and legal differences. I have outlined some of my home buying tips in the following ten points:

1. Always look for a real estate professional.

This is fairly obvious advice, coming from a real estate professional! But it is the first thing I would recommend when buying a home **overseas**. It could be a realtor, lawyer or a professional consultant, as long as they are an expert on the matter. This will help you to avoid headaches. Look at reputable websites when making your choice; a good professional will seem genuinely committed to informing homebuyers. You may be tempted to ask your aunt who lives in Colombia, an amateur real estate agent or your retired father's friend who says they have experience buying and selling their own homes and will help you save some money. However, an experienced professional will help you throughout the process and take the headache out of **property issues** (especially if you do not speak Spanish!). You can certainly do it all on your own, but think hard before committing to this course of action. As we say here in Colombia, "the cheapest thing turns out to be the expensive one" or, "You get what you pay for".

2. Information, Information, Information.

Gather accurate information about the **local market**, the local economy and whatever you need to help you feel **confident**. You don't need to become an expert in Colombia, but becoming familiar with some basic aspects will give you a general overview of how the home buying market works. Compare **prices**, know the best **areas**, interest **rates**, types of **construction**, etc. That's what this guide is about: providing the most valuable and informative content to help you make your decision.

3. Narrow down your location choices to just a few places.

You may be overwhelmed by hundreds of projects posted on the internet. Once you have a local overview, you can start **narrowing down** your choices. This is especially important in **big cities** like Bogotá or Medellin. In small towns like Bucaramanga it can be easier to choose. **Prioritize** what is important for you when making your home buying decision. Consider how close your workplace, schools, shops and amenities are. Make sure that surrounding properties are of a **similar standard** and size.

4. Think of the future resale value and whether it will make a good rental property.

This is especially important if you are buying for **investment purposes** or for temporary living. It is not necessarily the case that the bigger the house the easier to sell. In Colombia two- or three-bedrooms apartments have the best/quickest sell-on value. Also, a **big kitchen** is a must and two **bathrooms** are a plus.

5. Get some local legal advice.

Normally **notaries** can give you information about all of the related clauses included in a property deed. But for foreign buyers it may be be useful to obtain professional advice for real estate contracts, tax and overseas investment related issues. I have my own in-house legal staff experienced in sales contracts, title studies and real estate related issues. For tax, accounting and foreign investment related issues I work with an experienced legal group specializing in the setup of corporations, foundations and the handling of all types of real estate transactions.

6. Be sure of what you really want.

Sometimes we don't even know what we really want. But take your time to think about it. Make a priority list of your **home wishes**. Determine your housing needs. Apartment, house, studio, loft or condo? Is it a holiday home? A temporary home or an investment home?

How important are the amenities? Are you looking for short-term gain or regular long-term income? If you are buying for **investment purposes** it is important that you understand and are comfortable with the associated risk factors.

7. Stay focused. Don't waste your time.

You may be tempted to buy something that is not what you really need. You don't want to be wasting time viewing property that is wholly inappropriate or completely unaffordable. However, you should go looking for your home with an open mind. You'll soon realize that it is virtually impossible to find exactly what you want, so you may need to compromise on some issues and prioritize your requirements.

8. Stick to your budget.

Stay within your budget by considering what you want to buy and allowing for extra costs. Consider **future expenses** including maintenance fees (the more amenities the higher the maintenance fees, and the higher the number of units per community the lower the fees) and **taxes** (a higher strata pays more property tax).

9. Check tax and foreign investment laws.

Make sure you are aware of the relevant **foreign investment laws** and tax implications. It is easy to miss the **benefits** you may be eligible for as a foreign investor.

10. When you find a property negotiate the best deal.

Use the information you have acquired and always ask for a discount! When buying a home directly from the owner, they will tend to overvalue their property because the buyer always undervalues it. So, a seller will usually expect an offer lower than that listed for their property. The exception to this is if the asking price is followed by the words "not negotiable". For new developments and off-plan projects prices are fixed, but you can always negotiate financial discounts depending on the payment proposed.

COLOMBIAN REAL ESTATE INVESTMENT TIPS

Real estate investing activity in Colombia has provided stability, wealth and excellent returns for middle class Colombians, wealthy families and international investment funds.

As an area of obvious growth and potential, real estate investors in Colombia are confident that they will experience substantial financial gains as the demand for both commercial and tourist residential property in Colombia increases.

These are my four basics investing tips for real estate:

> *RULE No. 1: Always think about real estate investment, as a long-term investment.*

Why? Because as with any other type of investment, you can't predict the future. When you invest in real estate there is a level of risk involved because the market fluctuates constantly. Even if you just want to buy properties to flip, you have to keep this in mind. I consider flipping to be in the same category as the casino, and I don't consider myself a gambling type of guy.

You need to be prepared for market changes and as with any long-term investment you will need to be financially prepared to cover the costs required to sustain your investment, which should be recovered in the future sale of the property. There is no guesswork involved in real estate, but rather calculations of costs required to invest and what you will need to make to succeed. You need to be thinking about selling the property before you have even purchased it.

RULE No. 2: *Do your Homework. Be informed about the local real estate market.*

Once again: Information, information, information. You should begin by becoming familiar with the local real estate market because this is a direct indicator of the nation's real estate market. Gaining this information is vital to your success in real estate. The local economy is a huge determining factor when it comes to the market value of a property. If the local economy is up the price of a home goes up and vice versa when the economy drops. Many of the changes that occur in the market are caused by an increase in interest rates, tax rates and unemployment rates.

Another indicator to consider is the average time a house is on the market in a particular area. If homes are selling fast and their average market time is low, it is a good sign that the market is hot and could be profitable. An experience local real estate agent should be able to give you this information. They can also provide you with information about future developments in the area and potential changes in the land use. Real estate professionals hear things by word of mouth and may know about a future shopping mall, street widening works, etc.

RULE No. 3: *Define what you expect from your investment.*

Are you looking for an **investment property** or a rental **property**? You could buy an investment property and hope to cash in on the property in the future, or you could look for a rental property that will offer profitable cash flow from month to month.

For rental property you have two different values with the potential to increase. The property value and the rent value. You can rent an apartment in Colombia for about 0.5-1% of the property's commercial value. The average increasing value rate for real estate has been 10% for the last three years. So, you could get a minimum of 16% average return. Since banks pay a seven percent annual interest return for funds, this is not a bad deal.

Of course, there will always be other expenses that you must pay, including taxes and rental agent fees. However, these additional expenses will still leave a nice little cash flow of profit for your efforts.

As a property investor you must focus on the big picture. You will probably buy an investment property that allows you to make a good profit in approximately two or three years.

If you're planning to stick with it for a longer period and your house is in a hot market, you can expect a higher return for your investment.

When you are a property investor you will probably not be very interested in making money on your investment immediately. Your primary objective is to hold onto the property long-term and waiting to sell the property when the market value has risen significantly.

The best scenario for you will depend on your needs and your resources. If you have the time and money, then an investment property could be way to go, but if you need to have cash flow from your property then a rental property may be the best choice for you.

RULE No. 4: Investing in Hot Markets. Don't follow every trend.

Miami, Las Vegas, New York. In 2005 many people made a lot of profit in less than a year. When I started **investing and promoting** real estate in the US market in 2004, the value increasing rate in Miami was about 20-25% over several years and even the most respectable and experienced real estate investors predicted that the prices would continue rising. A lot of Colombian investors, including me, followed the cheery advice.

What happened? In 2006 prices stopped going up. What do you do when you have placed your only savings in a **down payment** and the closing date is at your heels? Well, if you're lucky enough you can retrieve the same down payment amount after two years. But if you can't close the property you will lose money.

So, we didn't stick to Rule No. 1 and of course we broke Rule No. 4. Don't follow a trend just because everybody else is.

Well, you might ask, how can you predict high or low increases in real estate market? Instead of following trends, it is wiser to look at the big picture (Rule No. 2).

At the end of 2005, there were already indications that interest rates were going to rise. In Colombia we saw the same situation in the early 1990's. A five year real estate boom with interest rates that scaled up at the end of the decade, leaving some buyers in serious trouble.

So, an important thing to be aware of is the direction of interest rates. As they fall, people can use loans to buy, demand increases and prices can easily rise.

Another good indicator is the rate of job creation in the area, which drives demand for housing and other real estate. A real estate boom may pass a city by if there is no growth in jobs, and therefore no growth in population.

However, the opposite is also true: it is much less likely that people will be able to continue to pay higher prices if interest rates are rising.

Ultimately, anyone can obtain the secret formula to success when buying a property abroad. If you can find the right property in the best location and grab it at the lowest price possible before it becomes common knowledge, congratulations! You have won the lottery!

STEP 1: CHOOSE THE PLACE

COLOMBIAN HOT SPOTS AND THE LOCAL REAL ESTATE MARKET

Bogota

Medellin

Bucaramanga

Cali

Barranquilla

Cartagena

Santa Marta

Villa de Leyva

BOGOTA: THE BIG CITY

Enjoy Bogota's urban renovation

When I talk about **Bogota** with my foreign friends, I always tell them that living in Bogotá is like living in any other capital city in the world with all the advantages and disadvantages of a **big city** at my disposal. However, Bogota is completely different from any other Colombian city. That's what it makes it special.

Like any other city, it has good and bad areas. When I was living in France, during my first trip to Paris I stayed in a low budget student's hotel at the 18th "arrondissement" and for me, the street (maybe one of the few of Paris) was similar to one I knew in downtown Bogotá.

I wasn't lucky with the hotel in Paris, but I can assure you that Bogotá and all Colombian cities are not the Hollywood image that many people have in their minds.

Forget the cheesy "Mr. and Mrs. Smith" movie with Brad Pitt and Angelina Jolie that shows a rural town among mountains with no buildings, streets mase of mud and no urban development. And definitely do your best to forget the "disco bar" with frightened chickens running all over the place!!

Bogotá has so much to offer. It has become one of the major cities in Latin America with a considerable amount of international taste. It is the primary destination for foreigners for obvious reasons. The country still has a very centralized structure, so if you want be nationally connected you need to settle down in Bogotá.

REAL ESTATE FACTS

After a period of high price increases, Bogotá prices entered a long period of adjustment after 2010s.

Property in the city's northeastern districts increased in value by an average of 25% per year in the boom period between 2003 and 2007, before prices leveled off.

The city's most expensive real estate is in this northeastern section, closest to the mountains that form a natural barrier to expansion on the eastern flank.

High-end units in new and predominantly red brick apartment buildings in the northeastern districts of **Rosales**, **Chicó**, **Parque 93**, **Santa Barbara, La Carolina** and Bosque Medina have the highest value in Bogota.

Strata is determined by blocks. So, don't be amazed to find houses with different stratification in the same neighborhood.

Obviously, there are some better areas than others, and the **distance between points** becomes an important issue when buying or renting a place to live.

I like to focus on those areas with the best living facilities that are more convenient for foreigners and areas where real estate development is concentrated in the city.

These are the north and northeastern parts of the city. However, feel free to ask me about the special area you want to know more about.

Northern areas

Cedritos
Chicó

Country
Santa Barbara
Chapinero Alto

Northeastern areas

Suba
Cerros de Suba
Niza and la Alhambra

Northern Surroundings Towns

In nearest surrounding towns at the north there are luxury complexes with comfortable country style houses. This area includes the rural areas of La Calera, Chia, Sopó, Cajicá and Briceño.

TAKE A SMALL BOGOTA TOUR AND PICK YOUR FAVORITE LOCATION

Undertaking a tour of Bogota to see all the **places you may want to live** could take you weeks. Perhaps you don't have that much time? You can get right to the point instead, with this short description of some of the best **areas in Bogotá** featuring good living facilities as starting point for your real estate search.

HOW TO LOCATE YOUR SURROUNDINGS

Start your city tour by locating yourself. The most common point of reference in Bogotá is the **East Mountains**. The city is flanked by mountains to the east and the airport is also located to the East. So, when you arrive in Bogota the first thing you should do is ask a taxi driver where the **Sanctuary of Monserrate** is and he'll point you to the East Mountains. Then you know you're going in the right direction.

The streets of Bogotá have been laid out in a grid pattern, which is a Spanish legacy. They are most often named with numbers. The *"Carreras"* (like avenues) run **parallel to the mountains** and they begin their count in ascending order from east to west. For example, Carrera 7th is close to the bottom of the eastern hills. You'll see abbreviations such as Cr, K and Crs.

The *Calles* (streets, in English) cross the *Carreras* perpendicularly and are counted in ascending order from **south to North**. You'll find abbreviations such as C, Cll and Cl. Others.

There are also *Diagonales*, which run diagonally east-west like the Calles; and the *Transversales,* which run diagonally but south-north. Avenues, abbreviated as Av, are usually larger than "Carreras". They are commonly identified by names like *Avenida Jimenez, Avenida Caracas, Avenida Circuvanlar*, etc. It can sound a little confusing! Don't worry, the only thing you really need to know is where you're standing and where you need to go, and you'll learn that it's not complicated at all.

BOGOTÁS POPULAR NEIGHBOURHOODS FOR FOREIGNERS

NORTH	NORTH EAST	DOWNTOWN AND SURROUNDINGS	EAST
Cedritos	Cerros de Suba	Centro Internacional	Ciudad Salitre
Chico	Colina Campestre	La Candelaria	La Soledad
Country	170 Street and surroundings	Santa Bárbara (Centro)	Castilla y Marsella
Santa Barbara			Centro Nariño
Chapinero	Niza y Alhambra		Engativá
Rosales	San Jose de Bavaria		Fontibón y Tintal
Santa Ana			Kennedy y Mandalay
La Cabrera			Metrópolis
			Nicolás de Federmán

CEDRITOS

Travels south to north from 134th Street to 170th Street, and West to East from 7th Avenue (Carrera Séptima) to the North Highway (Autopista Norte).

60% is strata four. The strata qualification ranges from one (the lowest) and six (the highest) and is a way to rate public utilities, and ensure that wealthiest sectors pay more to subsidize lower sectors.

It was traditionally a **residential community** (for upper-middle and average classes) combined with commercial activities. Its main road axes have a great commercial dynamic that offers all kinds of services and products. A particular advantage is the abundant existing road network in the area. It allows for easy traffic inside its perimeters and a fast mobilization toward other points of the city.

Real Estate Facts

Apartments for rent in strata three to four have the highest rotation. Rental prices increase their value on a 9% average, one of the highest in the city. The major real estate supply for brand new projects is at residential community buildings, with **two- and three-bedrooms apartments**. The peaceful environment and the urban infrastructure inside the neighborhoods provides the same comfort to residents as those in a higher strata.

Shopping Malls

Centro Comercial Cedritos.
Diagonal 151 No. 32-19
200 retail and services stores, eight movie theaters, two department stores, a children's playground, food court and casino.

Centro Comercial Mazuren
Autopista Norte No. 150-46
193 retail and services stores, banks and one department store.

Bilingual Schools

Fundacion Colegio de Inglaterra (English School)

Gimnasio Femenino

Colegio Anglo Colombiano

Colegio Anglo Francés Campestre

Colegio Princeton

Colegio Rochester

Colegio Thomas Jefferson

Colegio Santa Francisca Romana

Colegio Italiano Leonardo Davinci - (Italian)

Hospitals

Fundación Cardioinfantil
Cll. 163 a No. 28-60

Clínica Monserrat
Cll 134 No. 30-31

Clínica DEL NORTE
Cra. 22 No. 139-55

CHICÓ

Runs south to north from 72nd Street to 100th Street, and west to east from 7th Avenue (Carrera Séptima) to 15th Street.

70% of the population is in strata six.

This is the neighborhood of the famous **Parque de la 93**. It is the only area that people recommend in the forums as this was historically the **"navel of Bogotá"**. It is also one of my favorite areas in Bogotá as I have lived there in three different places.

It is considered one of the most **exclusives and traditional** areas for business and housing and also features the highest value increase. That's why it has a concentration of the better restaurants, bars, fashionable stores and other commercial services in Bogotá.

The best route on public transport is the **Transmilenio** route at the North Highway. Secondary routes are also easy but they require the normal public buses. The best option is to take a **"Bus ejecutivo"**. Otherwise, you will have an uncomfortable standing, overcrowded ride.

People living in the area enjoy large **shopping centers**, superstores and all kinds of medical, religious, recreational and educational services. There is also a great network of **biking routes** and parks that connect with other important areas of the city.

One of the issues in this zone is **traffic**. This is an issue all around Bogotá, but Chicó can make you crazy. You can find yourself stuck in peak hour (early in the morning, noon and end of the afternoon) traffic feeling that you are not moving at all,. You will need to be patient. Although the sector is surrounded by high arterial ways, they are not enough to support the high traffic that moves through Chicó.

Real Estate Facts

You can find luxury apartments for sale and for rent from between 90-300 square meters. The renting options for **business purposes** in skyscraper buildings with high-tech specifications are based on the most important road axes.

Four of the major business districts are centered at 72nd St (Avenida Chile), 82nd, 94th and 100th streets **(World Trade Center)**. In these areas there is a mix of residential living, hotels, banking and commercial establishments and **diplomatic headquarters**.

At 7th Avenue just beside the east hills you can find a luxury apartment complex with high amenity specifications (it's also the most expensive complex in the area).

Because of these characteristics corporate, commercial, and residential real estate in the area has a higher demand not only for national buyers but also for foreign investors. Consequently, the asking prices are high and have had more than a ten percent annual average for the last five years.

Shopping Malls

CENTRO ANDINO
200 exclusive retail and services stores, four movie theaters, Cine Bar, food court and Casino.

CENTRO COMERCIAL ATLANTIS
Calle 81 Carrera 14
A small shopping place with fancy stores, food court and Cinemark. At the ground level is the **Bogota's Hard Rock Café**.

CENTRO COMERCIAL GRANAHORRAR
Avenida Chile (Cll. 72) No.10-34
150 small retail and services stores, four movie theaters and a children's playground.

Restaurants and Bars

You will hear people to talk about the G, T or Pink Zone. Don't worry, these are not red-light districts. The **T Zone**, formerly known as the Pink Zone (*Zona Rosa*) is the area that features some of the best restaurants and bars in the city. It surrounds the Centro Andino mall between 82nd and 85th street. Sometimes people confuse the Zona Rosa area with 93 Park because they have the same type of places. Although they are separated by just a few blocks, if you try to travel between them by car at 10:00 p.m. it can take hours. Your best option is to find a centrally located parking spot and walk around freely.

At the **Zona G** you can find a variety of restaurants. Chinese, Italian, Colombian, light, French, Seafood, etc., all just a few steps from each other. This area is between 69th and 72nd streets and up 7th Avenue. The G Zone was named for "gourmet" and "gastronomy" and Zone T has its name because it is an intersection of two walking streets.

Bilingual Schools

Liceo Frances Louis Pasteur
Calle 87 No. 7-77

Colegio Nueva Granada
Cra. 2 Este No. 70-20

Hospitals

Clínica del Chicó
Carrera 21 No.90-59

Centro Médico Antiguo Country
Cra. 18 No. 84-10

Clinica Barraquer
Av. 100 No. 18A-51

Clinica del Country
Cr.16 No. 82-57

COUNTRY

Runs south to north from the 116th Street to the 134th Street, and west to east from 7th Avenue (Carrera Séptima) to the North Highway (Autopista Norte).

In the middle of this area, you can find the **Country Club**, a traditional private social community founded in 1917. Its facilities include 30 tennis courts, one for polo and two golf courses. The club has had a heavy influence on the wealthy development of the area. 100% of the population is in strata five and six. This is primarily a **residential neighborhood**.

In recent years there have been heated discussions between the inhabitants of the sector and the municipal government, because there is a public project to convert the Country Club into an open **public park**. There are a lot of economic and politic interests involved, but I think it is a daring proposal and not far off becoming reality.

Real Estate Facts

Apartments with more than 110 square meter areas in residential buildings; houses in closed communities with high specifications and social areas rule the sector's supply.

The **Unicentro mall** is located in this area. It was the first shopping mall in Colombia and is still one of the most important in Bogotá. Recently the international Spanish retail chain ZARA made a deal to open its first store in Colombia at a 1.200 square meter location at Unicentro. The property was valued at COP$20.000.000 per square meter! (About US$100 per square foot). Not bad for a mall that is more than 30 years old.

Shopping Malls

UNICENTRO

305 retail and services stores, two department stores. You can find whatever you need here. National and international stores, banks, eight movie theaters, children's playgrounds, travel agencies, restaurants, bowling, leather shops, art galleries, music stores and a Casino.

Bilingual Schools

Colegio Helvetia
Calle 128 No. 58-91

Hospitals

Clínica La Sabana
Av. 19 No. 102-71

Clínica El Bosque
Cll. 134 No. 12- 55

Clínica REINA SOFIA - SANITAS
Cra. 31 No. 125A – 23

SANTA BARBARA

In Santa Bárbara you can find one of the seven business districts of the city. The 116th street at 7th Avenue is the location where several national and international companies have their corporate offices. The Radisson Hotel and Hacienda Santa Barbara Mall are also here. 60% of the population is in strata six.

This area used to be the municipality of Usaquén, an old colonial town founded by Indian natives. Later it was absorbed by the city's expansive growth. Today, in its historical center – 119th street at Carrera 5^a – some evidence of the colonial and republican architecture remains. Painters, sculptors, jewelers, photographers and collectors of antiques live here. To the west are districts of elegant houses and apartments.

This is an oasis in the city. To get here, go via the north by the Carrera 7th, travel a few blocks ahead of the Hacienda Santa Barbara, cross to the left and travel straight up. Go into the tiny central park and have lunch at any of the restaurants there. You will enjoy the peace and quiet of this of country little town.

Real Estate Facts

This is an exclusive area where houses and apartments of generous areas characterize the real estate supply. The real estate market is focused on renting apartments of more than 100 square meters and the sale of luxurious houses to the upper classes. One of the urban characteristics of the area is the presence of several small parks or so called "green areas".

Shopping Malls

HACIENDA SANTA BARBARA
Carrera 7 No. 115-60
More than 300 retail and services stores, restaurants, supermarket, food courts, banks, etc. Its colonial architecture and open air style makes it one of my favorite areas. If you want to buy Colombian handcrafts this is the place to go. You can find a variety of jewelry, watch and silverware stores.

Hospitals

Fundacion Centro Medico Santafé
Cll 116 No.9-02

MEDELLIN: "A PARADISE ON EARTH"

Medellin is traditionally known as the **"City of the Eternal Spring"**. It has the privilege of being surrounded by **green mountains** which give the city year-round spring weather, great for any activity. The city's average temperature is 24° centigrade (74 °F).

It is well known all over the world for its **beautiful women**. The "paisitas" enchant with their particular way of talking.

It's also known as **"The Capital of the Flowers"**. Its traditional parade of "silleteros" at the annual "flowers fair" is one of the most beautiful events in the world.

I like Medellin because it is **not as big as Bogotá** but **not as small as Bucaramanga**.

So, if you are looking for a city with all the advantages of a big one, that is as friendly as a small one and has the perfect weather, don't think twice about Medellin.

REAL ESTATE FACTS

The market is very active and not speculative. As with any other real estate market, location is important. The advantage here is that any zone is a good location!

Most of the price appreciation witnessed in the city has been driven by stability in the local economy, a growing middle-class and Colombian expats living abroad and investing in Colombia.

Districts with the highest demand for living are:

In the south-east: El Poblado

(The Village) is the financial center of Medellin and without comparison, the area with the greatest concentration of wealth. It's fascinating to think that about 100 years ago the Prado Barrio used to be the where the wealthy lived and this can still be discerned via the old mansions in the neighborhood.

A special area within El Poblado is that surrounding Parque Lleras, situated between Hotel Park 10 and the Dann Carlton just up from Parque el Poblado, this is without a doubt the hub for nightlife, glossy bars and restaurants in Medellin. It is always packed at night on the weekends but alternatively is also a much quieter area to go during the day for lunch and you can wonder around or sip a coffee at the Juan Valdez café at the top of the park.

This area has the highest prices per square meter in the city. Prices in this area can be around 2-2.5 million pesos per square meter, or about USD $80-100 per sq. foot.

In the east: Laureles y Belén (Loma de los Bernal).

I found this to be a very beautiful and quiet neighborhood with lots of shops, restaurants and green areas. Laureles is a quiet neighborhood composed of upper-middle-class single-family residents and upscale apartment complexes. It has remained somewhat off the radar, but I know several Americans that have purchased apartments in Laureles over the past few months. Laureles is also very close to both Calle 33 and La 70, a popular hangout for young Colombians, especially at night. Those who are looking for something different from Parque Lleras might find Laureles interesting.

Set at a slightly lower altitude than El Poblado, Laureles is often noticeably warmer. Unlike El Poblado, it is also predominantly flat with plenty of sidewalks, although arguably less green.

Although it doesn't have a metro station, Laureles is well served by public transport. And, despite a swarm of high-rise condos and upmarket supermarkets, Laureles has many cheap restaurants and cafes.

Real estate prices in this zone are about 25% lower than they are in other neighborhoods like Poblado and Envigado.

At the North of Laureles is Bello. Bello is actually a city within a city and is comprised of 81 separate neighborhoods with mainly residential and mixed-use buildings. Bello is home to many furniture designers and manufacturers both big and small and many of its residents work in this industry.

Real estate prices in Bello are considerably lower than Laureles.

In the south: Envigado.

While El Centro can be too congested and polluted, or El Poblado too modern and almost boringly safe,

Envigado dabbles in **a little sophistication** while maintaining its traditional Colombian charm. It's a great place to sample some typical Colombian cuisine or check-out a laid-back salsa bar. Envigado is technically a city in its own right and has its own mayor, football team, newspapers, etc. Indeed, it feels a little distinct from other parts of Medellin and more like a typical South American city with lots of low-rise buildings and bustling streets of people.

Downtown:

Even though it can be fairly congested and hotter than other higher, fresher parts of town, there are a number of things worth seeing in downtown Medellin. **The Plaza Botero** has a sensational collection of statues donated by Fernando Botero himself. This, together with the Botero Museum is the main tourist attraction of Medellin. Urban renewal has taken place downtown and developers are offering some attractive projects there.

Metropolitan Area – El Retiro and Llanogrande:

Suburbs outside or near to the city are also a very good option for living. In LlanoGrande you can find country houses in safe and comfortable luxury housing projects. Areas like **El Retiro** are just 30 minutes by car and the **San Nicolas Valley** has a complete urban development with commercial, educational and health services.

BUCARAMANGA: A GREAT PLACE TO LIVE!

Well, what can I say about **Bucaramanga**? Everything!! It is the place where I was born and I live here very happily.

I had the opportunity to live in Bogotá for five years and in France for about a year-and-a-half, but I always returned and eventually realized that it's the best place to live for me. It's what we call in Colombia "*Un Buen vividero*" - **a great place to live**.

It's the kind of town where you can still go home to have lunch and take a little **nap** before going back to work. Everything is nearby so you don't have to worry about **long distances** or crowded traffic. Having said this, you do not need a car as you can move around the city in comfortable inexpensive taxis or using the "Metrolinea", a fast public transport system (just like TransMilenio in Bogotá, which you can use to move between the north and south).

Bucaramanga combines nice weather, (26 °C average, 75 ° F), great commercial facilities and boasts the most advanced **heart disease treatment** clinic in Latin America (*Fundacion Cardivascular de Colombia*). It also has the most important research center for the Colombian **oil industry** (*Instituto Colombiano del Petroleo ICP*).

Its privileged location surrounded by outstanding areas of **forest and mountains** makes it an obligatory pass from the center of the country to the **Caribbean coast**.

It's also near to several different types of landscapes. From here, I can visit the east within one hour by car to reach the **Páramo de Berlin** (4° C) and spend a cold weekend in a wooden cabin drinking hot brandy next to a fireplace. If the cold isn't your scene, **La Mesa de los Santos** and its year-round spring weather (16 ° C) is just 25 minutes away.

Or, I can journey to the south and within 45 minutes I'm at the **Chicamocha Canyon** (30° C) where I can go hiking and enjoy the marvelous landscape and views, or I can keep driving another hour and I'm in the town of **San Gil** next to the Fonce River, a perfect place to do some rafting.

You might thing I spend my time catching a cold for all of the changing weather! But really, what I'm trying to say is that this kind of diversity could be on your doorstep.

From here you can take a safe trip by car to:

- **The Caribbean coast**: Santa Marta 8 h Barranquilla 9 hours, Cartagena 10 hours.

- **Bogota**: 7 hours.

- **Medellin**: 6 hours

- **Cúcuta and Venezuelan border**: 5 hours

- **Eje cafetero**: 10 hours (making a stop in Ibague)

- **Villa de Leyva**: 7 hours

It takes no more than two hours to reach any other Colombian city by plane.

REAL ESTATE FACTS

Bucaramanga is the capital of the **Santander** province to the east of the country and it lies in the beautiful valley of the **Río de Oro**, or "River of Gold". Enclosed by gold mines already established by local Indian tribes, the town was founded on a plateau (**La Meseta**). As the gold in the nearby mines petered out, agriculture and other industries came to the fore.

All of its urban development was undertaken at La Meseta. Downtown and the most traditional neighborhoods are located there. Over the years the city has extended toward some nearby towns, forming the **metropolitan area** (Bucaramanga Giron, Florida and Piedecuesta). Bucaramanga has a majority middle-class population. You will see a harmonious mix of buildings and construction. Maybe that's why it is called **"The**

Pretty City"!

The city hasn't missed out on the country's **real estate boom**. Projects for every kind of budget with great specifications are taking place all over the city.

Real estate prices in Bucaramanga have grown steadily – the average valuation in the last five years is 18% and new commercial developments including hypermarkets and shopping centers are under construction.

Residential areas with the highest demand are:

At the Meseta

Cabecera

El Prado

La Aurora

Lagos del Cacique

Los Pinos

Ciudadela Real de Minas

Conucos

To the South

Cañaveral

Menzuly Valley

Ruitoque Condominio; the community I'm very happily living in.

RUITOQUE GOLF CONDOMINIO: WHERE YOU CAN STAY CONNECTED TO NATURE

Let me talk about the place where **I live** since 2006. *Ruitoque Golf Condominio* was the **first** of its kind in this country. People from other cities who come here agree with me on this. It began 15 years ago and in the past few years similar projects following the same philosophy have gained in popularity in other Colombian cities.

It is a residential **community** complex only 30 minutes away from the city's downtown, developed at the **"Mesa the Ruitoque"** (Bucaramanga's "second floor"). It is projected to host approximately 1,350 family units. The weather is always around 19° C to

20°C and in the rainy season falls to a minimum of 12°C.

What most attracted me (and likely everyone else!), was its **natural environment**. More than 190 ha (470 acres) of a total of 500 ha (1.235 acres), including its spectacular **golf course** was designed by Jack Nicklaus' Firm.

Your backyard can feature the spectacular diversity of **bird species**. I don't know much about the subject, but I would consider Ruitoque to be a **birdwatching** paradise. Colombia is one of the most important places for birdwatchers, and every day I found a new kind of **colorful** birdie in my yard.

Close to the Ruitoque golf course there are about six different spots to practice **paragliding**. With 300 flying days a year, this is considered one of the best paragliding **sites** in Colombia. I'm not a regular participant, but am waiting for my website to run itself so I can make it an everyday activity!

Golf, **paragliding**, **outdoors activities**. There are few places where you can get it all in one. When I started **building** my home in 2006, I was worried about changing my normal habits. My kids had to get up earlier in the morning to go to school, have lunch in the city instead of at home, no naps, etc. Now I get up early to enjoy the sunrise, I prefer to go jogging instead of napping, and I would like to have more time to play golf, practice paraglide or mountain biking.

Many people from **Europe and the US** have realized that they can enjoy a **quality of life** at Ruitoque Golf that is equal to or even better than what they have access to back home. It is at a much lower cost, and some have decided to buy a home or even build one. This might sound like it is only for the wealth or a small minority. Even though it is not the kind of place that everybody in Colombia can afford, the people who live here are a variety of professionals, from hard working **entrepreneurs** to university professors (my neighbor teaches at the State University).

You can find houses at Ruitoque Golf Condominio from USD $200,000 to USD $1,000,000 and higher. There are also **lots** available at about US$500 square meter where you can build a house of your own whilst keeping the same **architectural design** in the frontage. Within the complex there are 19 different **communities** and each one has a diverse architectural design. The area per houses varies from 300 to 800 square meters, or more.

As there are limited number of units, the secondary real estate market is very active. There are a lot of **investors** that bought in at a very good price and now they want to sell. People interested in buying made a very **good deal** at the time.

SANTA MARTA: MY FAVORITE VACATION PLACE!

Santa Marta, on Colombia's Caribbean coast is the **oldest Hispanic** city in the country, although it doesn't have the architectural beauty of Cartagena.

Instead, it has better natural locations and archaeological spots. It has great beaches, white sand, a better climate and outstanding landscapes. The capital of Magdalena State, it is probably one of the most visited domestic tourist destinations in the country. Its hotel infrastructure, the white sand beaches and natural parks, between which is the **Tayrona Park** and the majestic **Sierra Nevada**, gives the city a very privileged location.

It has a year-round tropical climate. It is hot during the day, but the evening **sea breezes** are cool and make sunsets and nightlife particularly appealing. Santa

Marta and the nearby beaches have the **warmest tropical sea** in the world.

It has been my favorite place to spend **family vacations** since my childhood. It's now my kids' favorite, too. We try to plan our vacations at least six months in advance because, like us, many other Colombians also vote it their favorite place.

Hotel developments stretch far to the south of the city and beyond the north, about 40 km.

If you are traveling by car from the countryside you'll reach the following areas at the south part of the city:

- **Piedra Hincada** Area (**Puerto Galeon** and surroundings): has some small and artificial beaches.

- **Pozos Colorados** area: you can find the best hotel infrastructure here. It includes the **Irotama Resort and Marina, Zuana Beach Resort, Decameron and Santamar hotels and the convention center**. The sea in this area is ideal for sky and nautical sports.

- **El Rodadero**: the most overcrowded spot is a close-by picturesque resort town with the highest concentration of tourists in the high season. It has the widest beach but it is not as clean as the one in Pozos Colorados. In high season it's a kind of "spring break" environment. There are hotels in all price ranges, suitable for all kinds of budgets.

Within the city itself there is are no particularly good hotel offers. At the **Malecon** or **La Playa** Avenue in front of Santa Marta's Bay you can enjoy a **great sunset** view, but the beach in the city is not particularly nice.

Cruise ships make this a port of call, in addition to the commercial port.

Best beaches to visit:

- ✓ **Cañaveral-Arrecifes** in Parque Tayrona: fantastic beaches where you can find "eco-habs" and a camping-zone.
- ✓ **Playa Cristal**
- ✓ **Neguanje and Bahia Concha:** great beaches with picturesque restaurants run by locals.
- ✓ **Taganga:** a fishing village on a beautiful bay surrounded by mountains and soft, deep waters great for scuba diving.
- ✓ **Playa Grande**

Other tourist spots:

✓ **Ciudad Perdida, the "Lost City,":** the home of the Tayrona Indians was built on the lush slopes of the Santa Marta mountains between the 11th and 14th centuries. Thought to be larger than Machu Picchu, it was found and rescued from tomb raiders in the 1970's by Colombian archeologists.

✓ **"Quinta de San Pedro Alejandrino"**: the hacienda where Simon Bolivar died.

REAL ESTATE FACTS

Cartagena and Santa Marta have become the best **international spots** for real estate.

Real estate development hasn't moved as fast as in other Caribbean coastal cities. The completion of two important shopping centers in the city has also introduced a **new dynamic** to the real estate market in the city.

Over the last decade Santa Marta has grown and consolidated its urban development, taking advantage of its privileged natural environment that includes the sea, forest, rivers and Sierra Nevada all in one place.

This has created enormous potential for the development of eco-hotels and hotels, the building of second homes and hotels between El Rodadero and the airport and the arrival of a wide range of hotels from international chains (Marriot, Decameron and Sonesta, among others. These seek not only the sun and beaches, but also business, nature tourism, agrotourism, cultural tourism, ethno-tourism and ecotourism.

The urbanization process has accelerated over the past five years with a strong demand for the construction of housing and the development of buildings for commercial, service and institutional activities.

The main cities in the Colombian Caribbean (Santa Marta, Barranquilla, Cartagena) represent a market equivalent to approximately 25,000 housing units per year, with Santa Marta seeing the least development but the greatest growth potential.

Local developers agree that this is the best moment for high end project developments as the city has awakened to the demand for well-located houses and large, comfortable apartments.

Despite the condominium and hotel expansion, **luxury projects** are also under construction, especially in neighborhoods like Buenavista, next to the Manzanares river estuary and the single family homes at **El Jardin and Bavaria**.

CALI: THE HEAVEN'S BRANCH OFFICE

Cali is Colombia's **third largest city** and a center for sugar, coffee and textile industry. It is located in Colombia's southwestern region, about 995 meters above sea level and is the capital of the **Valle del Cauca** state, a diverse region of coast, foothills and the Andean cordillera.

A popular salsa song states that as long as New York is the capital of the world and Paris the city of light, Cali is the heaven's branch office.

It enjoys a terrific nightlife in the **salsotecas** and visitors can enjoy the historic center as well as excursions into the surrounding areas for sugar baron haciendas and the prime archaeological sites of **San Agustin and Tierradentro** that are located just a couple of hours away.

The City normally has two dry seasons, from December to March and again between July and August. The average temperature is 23° C (73.4°F)

It is famous throughout Latin America for its annual fair. **La Feria de Cali** runs from December 25 through to New Year's Eve and is famous for its cavalcade parade, bullfight season, and of course the salsa festival. The town becomes the world salsa capital and enjoys the most important salsa groups from around the world.

Fania All Stars, Gran Combo de Puerto Rico and Sonora Ponceña are some of the most famous artists that have performed here. **Hector Lavoe,** the famous Puerto Rican singer, fell in love with Cali and lived here for six months in 1982. It's an event that **Salsa lovers** can't miss.

Salsotecas abound on the northern side of the **Pance river**, particularly in the suburb of Juanchito. Night tours in "Chivas" – the colorful open wooden bus – last about five hours and will get you into a number of **salsa hotspots**.

Caleños used to be known as an example of civism. I say, "it used to" because in the later years the national perception was that city suffered from a "social breakdown", and that it lost the values that distinguished it as a **"Civic town"**. Fortunately, the local authorities and the Caleños themselves want to leave the unfair legacy that drug lords curated in the 1980's and 90's behind and they are working to recover the city's civic values.

REAL ESTATE FACTS

As in the rest of the country, local real estate sales are **increasing** steadily. The city is enjoying a good moment concerning real estate supply. Unlike other cities, however, **prices haven't increased** too much because there is still a lot of land available for construction.

Developers have bet on the supply of high-end properties, using the presale system that it is common all over the country. The **mid class housing projects** supply has also not diminished.

The highest prices are located in the **south**, where the value of the square meter reaches the COP$2.4 million per square meter. In the west, where land available for construction is limited, the price is similar, about COP$2.3 million per square meter.

CALI'S NEIGHBORHOODS

At the south
Ciudad Jardin

This continues to be an area in high demand. Some schools and universities are located here. Many people are moving from the north to the south searching for a country lifestyle that is near the city, which is why this is the area where the city has expanded.

About five minutes away, moving south along the route to Jamundí, you can find country projects with luxury characteristics. They are commonly supplied as plots of land of 1,200 square meters areas.

Shopping Centers
La 14 supermarket at Valle del Lili
Unicentro

At the North
Chipichape Shopping center

At the West
This is the traditional and wealthiest part of the city. You will find big apartments of 350, 230 and 150 square meters. There is not a good view of the city, but there are good views of the Dagua Canyon, Cristo Rey and Tres Cruces hills.

Normandía is another exclusive sectors but unlike the south, land availability is diminished.

Panorama Shopping center

Downtown
Centro Comercial Centenario

BARRANQUILLA: COLOMBIA'S GOLDEN GATE

Barranquilla is located at the Caribbean Sea estuary of Colombia largest river, **Magdalenas' River**, .

The city has historically attracted foreign people from around the world because of its port. That's why it was named "Colombia's Golden Gate". Its commercial development in the beginning of the 20th century brought **immigrants** mainly from Arabia, Syria, Lebanon, Germany and also the U.S, Italy and Spain.

The town is just between Cartagena and Santa Marta and less than an hour from both. The climate is rather hot with an average temperature of 29°C. However, at the end of the year the Alisios' winds cool it to a more **comfortable temperature**.

The rainy season is from May to June, and the city is popular because the streets flood like rivers, causing traffic chaos. I've always heard that it is a problem in the city's sewer system networks. Anyway, you need to be aware of this so that you don't get trapped in the middle of one of these rivers.

The most famous Colombian carnival takes place here. **Carnaval de Barranquilla's** parties in February feature the most popular tropical music bands from around Colombia and the world. It is considered the second largest Carnival of Latin America because of its cultural richness, but it doesn't have the same sexual connotation as the Carnaval de Rio in Brazil.

At the traditional *"Batalla de las Flores"* (battle of flowers) parade, the procession will walk through the city from the **South to North** until they reach Via 40 Avenue next to the Magdalena River, where everybody can join to dance and party.

REAL ESTATE FACTS

The capital of the Atlantic area has the cheapest square meter amongst the four main Colombian cities (Bogotá, Medellín and Cali).

The completion of commercial construction (supermarkets and shopping centers) is starting to **push real estate** developments in areas towards the north and to the south.

This is the reason the city has attracted the attention of multinational **retail chain** companies who want to feature in shopping center facilities.

For example, the five-year-old **Buenavista** Shopping center will be enlarged within a complementary project titled **Buenavista 2**.

Other projects under construction include: **Panorama,** which is located to the south-east and another with no name yet defined which is targeted at the middle-class population and located to the south of the city over the ancient road that goes to Cartagena.

There is also the French retail chain store **Carrefour at 30th street**; the enlargement of the Super Almacen Olimpica SAO at 53rd street; and existing areas including Villa Country, Country Plaza, Gran Centro, Exito and Parque Central.

In Barranquilla the construction business has had an important turnaround over the past five years. Development of **luxurious projects** has skyrocketed, particularly in the north of the city. Many important developers have undertaken construction projects in exclusive **neighborhoods** like The Golf, Altos de Ríomar, Alto Prado and residential districts like Paseo la Castellana and Buenavista. The majority are large apartments with just a few house offers.

Most of these projects have excellent finishes including porcelain polished tiles, granite countertops, 2.5 meter high ceilings, all-in-one kitchens and all sorts of amenities.

Unlike other Colombian cities, the offer of country-side projects in surrounding areas is not numerous. There are some developments on the road that leads from the city to the nice spot of **Puerto Colombia**.

CARTAGENA: THE HOTTEST REAL ESTATE MARKET IN COLOMBIA

Cartagena is a **world-class** location. It is **romantic, magical and glamorous**. You can ask Mel Gibson, Julio Iglesias or Mick Jagger how they felt there. Mick Jagger used to walk around the streets and nobody realized. Now everybody (including me) is waiting when for his next vacation!

It is by far the **best colonial city in America**. Just walk around its beautiful colonial streets and you will be sure to come back many times. It has romantic balconies, the sound of the sea and a soft breeze, making it the ideal place for honeymooners and lovers.

Declared a World Heritage location by UNESCO, the **"Walled City"** has all the ingredients for an extraordinary place to live: a colonial city enclosed within stone fortifications, **cultural** richness, modern and **luxurious hotels**, beautiful **beaches**, restaurants for all tastes and a vibrant **nightlife**.

So, it's not a secret that the **"Corralito de Piedra"** is attractive to international visitors. People from around the world have purchased and renovated some of the city's older homes. Now, the offer of ancient buildings is scarce, causing **prices** to scale up.

REAL ESTATE FACTS

Cartagena is **having a boom** in the real estate market. People from all over the world, especially Europeans, are starting to buy properties here. Also, Colombians living abroad want to buy a place to spend their **vacations**. Even I have to admit to renting an apartment six months in advance for our end-of-the-year vacation trip!

In some areas **prices** are starting to reach the same level as other **international hotspots** like **Punta Cana**, **Panama** or even **Miami**. Buildings from 15 to 50 stories high with exclusive designs and front sea projects have equal or even better characteristics than those in international hot spots.

Districts like **Boca Grande**, **El Castillo**, **El Laguito** and La **Boquilla corredor** (in front of Las Américas hotel), have the best variety of luxury real estate projects.

Tourism is concentrated in the **Boca Grande** district, a beachfront peninsula that gradually becomes the **El Laguito** Peninsula. This area has the most modern construction, including many modern hotels. It has modern shops, cyber-cafes, espresso bars, restaurants and a large, pleasant beach.

Another interesting neighborhood is **Manga**, just few minutes outside the old Cartagena. It is recognized for its **Republican** architectural house **style**. Although it doesn't quite have the excitement of the old city, it also doesn't have the annoying things like loud music at 2am or the throngs of tourist everywhere.

For those who simply want to live quietly in Cartagena, there are also apartment offers of 150 or 200 square meters (2 or 3 bedrooms) in residential areas with all types of commercial and transport **facilities**.

Projects with **swimming pools, children's playgrounds, saunas, gyms and spas**, are also affordable on all kind of budgets.

PLACES TO DO SOME SHOPPING

Caribe Plaza

In the traditional neighborhood of Pie de la Popa, this shopping center boasts the most ambitious commercial project of the Caribbean Coast.

It features 173 commercial and retail stores and the popular department stores Homecenter, Playland and the French retail chain Carrefour.

Paseo de la Castellana

Located in the middle of Pedro de Heredia avenue this is the biggest and most important shopping area in the city.

Los Ejecutivos and La Plazuela

Located very near residential areas and popular neighborhoods.

Bocagrande shopping center

In the tourist area of Bocagrande, in full Avenue San Martin, they also stand out as the business center of Bocagrande.

El Pueblito

Smaller than Paseo de la Castellana or Caribe Plaza but with a variety of services.

VILLA DE LEYVA: HISTORICAL AND COLONIAL JEWEL

Villa de Leyva is a perfectly preserved colonial-era town just 2.5 hours distance by car from Bogotá at the north, in the Andean mountains.

Declared a national historic monument in the 1950s, the town is a popular attraction and home to many artisans and famous Colombians.

It is considered by most local and foreign tourists to be an incredibly beautiful colonial town, with decent tourist infrastructure yet not overrun by tourism just yet.

You can easily see the entire village in a few hours, but you'll want to hang out here longer. The cobblestoned streets are difficult to ride on but lend themselves to a strolling tour of the colonial architecture featuring white-washed houses with wooden shutters, doors and balconies.

You can also elect to stay in a finca or farm. Make sure you make your reservations early for weekends in the high season and for major holidays.

Restaurants offer local favorites, fast food choices and international cuisine. There are also vegetarian restaurants and if you trust your stomach, you can try some of the local fast food snack offerings from street vendors.

Leyva (as most locals call the town) has been almost perfectly preserved: cobblestone streets, red-tiled roofs, whitewashed houses and balconies and private courtyards that retain the town's heritage. The town is small but the surrounding area will make you want to stay and enjoy hiking and camping options.

The weather is nice (fresh at night, 18 degrees Celsius average).

Most tourists here are Colombians from Bogota (on the weekend the streets, restaurants, places to stay and shops are crowded). During the week you'll find the town is nice and quiet.

You will also find a lot of foreigners (Germans, French and Americans, among other nationalities) who have chosen Villa de Leyva as their retirement home. Elvis Presley's drummer Bill Lynn was one of the famous residents of the town, and it was here he spent his last days.

It has been used also as a location for the filming of various TV and motion picture projects. Klaus Kinski chose the town as location for his film "Cobra Verde" in 1986.

THINGS TO DO IN THE SURROUNGING AREA

Horseback-riding (with a guide) for a couple of hours in the nearby Candelaria desert, which also has crystal blue lagoons (Pozos Azules) that you can take a dip in.

There is a beautiful area some 40 mins away from Villa de Leyva that features cascading waterfalls called "La Periquera".

Hiking in the surroundings is great, and you can go camping too.

It is also an area of paleontological richness. There is a famous tourist attraction called "El Fosil", a reasonably complete kronosaurus fossil, also known as a 120-million-year-old prehistoric marine reptile resembling an overgrown crocodile. The fossil is seven meters long (the animal was about twelve meters long but its tail hasn't survived). It's a baby kronosaurus (the adult animals were far larger) and it remains in the place where it was found.

Villa de Leyva's is one of the safest areas in Colombia and its most distinct feature is a huge cobblestoned plaza in front of the parish church. The Plaza Mayor is the largest of its kind in Latin America.

REAL ESTATE FACTS

According to figures from the real estate market in Colombia, although the construction and sale of houses in warm places such as Cartagena, Barranquilla, Santa Marta and Medellín are desired because of their proximity to the sea or because they are large cities, the need to find a location with a temperate climate without low humidity is now gaining ground in buyers' preferences.

This trend points easily to the popularity of Villa de Leyva, which has one of the most stable and pleasant climates (with minimal humidity and no mosquitoes!) near Bogotá.

In Villa de Leyva a dry and very pleasant desert environment coexists alongside a forest with native exotic trees, creating the perfect environment to disconnect from life in the polluted city.

The new housing projects in Villa de Leyva are based on respecting the colonial architectural style of the municipality whilst adapting it strategically to suit modern styles and lifestyle requirements.

It is important to keep in mind and review the rules on construction and remodeling, known as the Basic Plan of Territorial Ordering (PBOT, for its Spanish acronym). When choosing a property to build or remodel, there may be restrictions depending on its location and land use. You should also inquire about the availability of aqueduct services, as there are several options.

Once you have chosen a property, request a title study. It is common in the region to find properties with the legal figure of rights and actions, or properties with liens for possession.

STEP 2: CHOOSE THE PROPERTY

HOW TO BUY OFF-PLAN PROJECTS IN COLOMBIA

WHAT TO TAKE INTO CONSIDERATION WHEN LOOKING FOR OFF-PLAN PROPERTY AND AT THE PRE- CONSTRUCTION PHASE IN COLOMBIA.

Preconstruction properties in Colombia (also known as off-plan projects) generally refer to all new developments that are sold before the completion of the construction of the property and not, as it used to be, only properties in the initial pre-construction stage.

The buyer only has the property plans and renders provided by the developer as guidance for the finished property.

One of the biggest **differences between a resale property and new properties in Colombia is the seller**. Off-plan properties or new developments are sold directly by the developer whereas traditional resale properties are normally sold by a private owner.

The standard of developers in Colombia can be very different and as you will not be able to see the finished property before you have signed the contract it is highly recommended that you obtain further advice before committing to a new development.

Another difference between off-plan and resale properties is how the price is set.

The concept driving off-plan properties is that the developers are interested in selling as many properties as possible in a new development before they start the building work.

This helps the developer finance part of the project and is a good guarantee for their creditors. To attract as many early buyers as possible the price level is initially set below the market value so that both the early buyers and the developer benefit from this situation.

During the construction period, which normally takes from one to two years for housing projects and three to five years for tourism or commercial projects, the pricing level of the properties which have not been sold will increase until at the end of the construction they are equal to the market value.

As property prices in **Colombia have had an average increase for the latest ten years of about 5.6% per year** *(Source: DANE Departamento Nacional de Estadistica)*, the value of a property purchased in the initial stage of the pre-construction launch will have increased by the average increase of property price during the years of the construction.

DOCUMENTS ISSUED WHEN BUYING OFF-PLAN PROJECTS

1. Pre-Contract or Reservation Agreement

The first contract is the reservation contract, in which you pay a down payment of a small amount normally between three to five million pesos (about 2,000 to 5,000 US dollars) to take the property off the market and give the buyer enough time to obtain the outstanding amount needed to sign the promise of purchase agreement.

The date for the signing of the promise of purchase agreement is confirmed in the reservation contract and is normally one month later. If the buyer doesn't show or changes their mind about the property, the money paid upon reservation will be lost. The amount to be paid upon the signing of this contract is normally between 20-30% of the total property price and this contract will also confirm the amount that has to be paid during the construction period (the difference between the money paid at the reservation and private contract and the money available in mortgage, which is normally about 70%).

2. Trusteeship Agreement – Encargo Fiduciario

The trusteeship - similar to an escrow account in the US - is a financial body used by developers and offered in off-plan projects so that buyers can pay their monthly payments to a trustee during the construction period. This financial institution manages the resources and verifies that the sales and progression of the construction work corresponds to the dates and terms outlined by the project.

The trustee agreement document is not the promise of purchase agreement used for properties that are already built, but is instead a contract that regulates the way the money will be invested during the implementation of the project followed by the purchase of the property.

It is important to keep in mind that the trusteeship agreement is not signed by the developer executing the project, but by a trustee or escrow which will manage the aforementioned resources and make the disbursements to the builder only under the following conditions:

- The developer can sell a certain number of units within the real estate project, this is called the "break-even point" (between 40-60% of sales). This will be established in the trusteeship agreement.

- Once this "break-even point" is reached the buyer and developer must sign the promise of purchase agreement so that the trustee can undertake the disbursement of money and the developer can start building works.

- If the developer does not reach the aforementioned break-even point, i.e., they cannot sell the units agreed in the contract, the trustee can choose to return the money back to the potential buyer or investor, in accordance with the provisions of the contract trust.

> **Remember:** *Signing a trusteeship agreement is quite different from signing a promise of purchase agreement. You're undertaking a business investment for the purchase of a home which may or may not take place depending on whether the developer meets all stated conditions.*

Be careful when reviewing the trusteeship agreement before signing, as in some cases in the terms of reimbursement contracts may include penalties of 10% retention value on money deposited. In any case the fiduciary should pay a yield on that money.

Since the project is yet to be constructed the possibility of modifying the conditions initially laid down remains, but if the potential buyer or investor does not agree with the changes that the project undergoes, there is no obligation to honor the agreement and the buyer can claim back the value of their investment according to the terms of the trusteeship agreement (*see Graphic 1*).

RECOMMENDATIONS TO TAKE INTO ACCOUNT FOR THE TRUSTEESHIP AGREEMENT

To avoid future misunderstandings and headaches, take the time to read all the pages and fine print of the trusteeship agreement, and be sure it covers aspects such as:

- A clear indication that it is a fiduciary and not a promise of purchase agreement.
- The requirements (including deadlines) that must be met before the disbursement of resources to the developer. Also, the description of the process for delays or extended terms that may be required by the developer.
- The penalty amount (or percentage), if relevant, to be applied if either party terminates the contract.
- Detail of costs, deductions, and the terms of repayments if conditions are not met.
- The full description of the boundaries, specifications, areas and the location of the property. Provide written evidence if specifications are changed.
- The possibility that the technical and financial conditions can change, given written notice.
- In case of quotations for specific items, legal articles, etc., the entity must submit a copy of them so that the recipient is fully documented.
- Confirmation that the money should be given only to the fiduciary and that the developer or

its agents are completely prevented from receiving any type of payment. Violating this statement leads to legal sanctions being applied to the developer.

- Every month, the client must receive a bank statement with the ratio of the yields of their subscriptions.

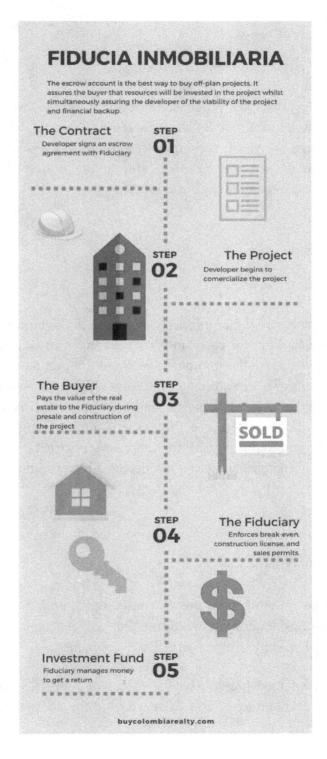

FIDUCIA INMOBILIARIA

The escrow account is the best way to buy off-plan projects. It assures the buyer that resources will be invested in the project whilst simultaneously assuring the developer of the viability of the project and financial backup.

The Contract
Developer signs an escrow agreement with Fiduciary

STEP 01

STEP 02

The Project
Developer begins to comercialize the project

The Buyer
Pays the value of the real estate to the Fiduciary during presale and construction of the project

STEP 03

SOLD

STEP 04

The Fiduciary
Enforces break-even, construction license, and sales permits.

Investment Fund
Fiduciary manages money to get a return

STEP 05

buycolombiarealty.com

89

3. Promise of purchase agreement

The promise of purchase agreement is the written document in which both parties define the terms of the negotiation with it subsequently serving as a model for the final deed. See detailed information in **step #5** of this guide for more information.

THINGS TO BEAR IN MIND WHEN BUYING NEW PROPERTY IN COLOMBIA.

As with any other property purchase it is important when looking for off-plan properties that you take into consideration the reasons you wish to purchase the property. This is especially important if you are looking to buy in the early stages of the development as you will not be able to see the property until a long time after you have signed the purchase contract. For a clearer picture, we have divided the buyers into four groups:

1. Investors

As an investor there are two important things to take into consideration to make sure that you get the highest return possible from an off-plan investment.

As explained previously, the prices of properties in a new development will increase during the construction period and they are initially set to below market value to attract early buyers. It is therefore important to buy as early as possible after the market launch of a new development - but this is not the only factor to be aware of.

In addition to focusing on the initial price it is also very important to take into consideration who is going to buy the property and what they are looking for. Although you may buy a cheap property, if you are not able to resell it before the completion of the development a big part of your potential profit may be lost.

People buying resale properties are normally private buyers looking for a holiday home or a place to settle down and as an investor you will need to take their preferences into account. Some investors incorrectly think that the cheaper the development, the more money they will earn. As most potential buyers of resale property are looking for a good quality property with certain characteristics the investor needs to take this into account before investing in a development.

2. Rental Property

If the main purpose of buying a property is to rent it out as a holiday home, there are a number of things to consider. First of all, the price of the property is more important than the quality of the development. Rental properties are damaged much faster than private properties and the features do not have to be luxurious – although, there will be a good relation between quality of the property and the rental price. As a buyer you do not have to focus as much on the quality of the development (i.e., as an investor does) and to get the lowest purchase price available it is recommended to buy as early in the development phase as possible.

Another aspect to take into consideration is the location and availability of nearby utilities. People renting a holiday home like to have services nearby including a supermarket, restaurants and bars, with other attractions including a golf course, a town center or the beach.

For the highest yearly return a golf course is a good option as golfers play throughout the year and it is then possible to rent out the property for a large number of weeks.

3. Settle Down in Colombia

As the property is going to be allocated for private use and likely for a longer time period, the quality and the aesthetic of the finished property are very important. Most people who buy a live-in property prefer to be able to see how it will look before signing a contract and paying part of the property price. Although there will be many plans and descriptions of the property available, your mental picture of the finished property will not always be identical to the reality. Therefore, it is recommended that buyers do not purchase a property in the initial phase of development and, where possible, that they view a finished show flat or at least the main structure of the property. Some developments offer the option to purchase a second or later phase of the development, allowing the buyer to see how the first phase has turned out.

It is important to take into consideration that you will be living there all year around and will therefore need certain utilities nearby like shops, doctors, schools, work and leisure activities, which are different to holiday maker requirements. You might like the area from previous vacation trips but to live in the area permanently may require additional amenities.

4. Holiday Home

Most people who buy a holiday home in a new development have a secondary intention. This could be to rent it out while they are not using it, to settle down within a few years or as a long-term investment.

If the main purpose is to use the property as a private holiday home the finished property has to meet a minimum of desired qualities. However, the quality will have an important impact on the price and the buyer must set some realistic goals according to the money they are willing to spend. Sometimes you can find the perfect property a little further inland or in another province where the prices are typically lower.

In any case, with this type of purchase it is recommended that the buyer purchases a little later in the construction phase as although the prices will not be as cheap as in the initial launch, they will be able to see how the finished property will look making a decision.

As the main use of the property is for a holiday home you will have think about the utilities available at the location. On a vacation most people want to relax and have fun and if you have preferred leisure activities it is a good idea to make sure they are nearby, so you do not have to spend a large part of your vacation in a car.

THE PROS OF OFF-PLAN PROPERTY INVESTMENT

- ✓ By buying an off-plan property today you are securing the price of that property at today's prices. By the time the property is completed it may very well have risen in value, thus making a significant return on your investment immediately. Furthermore, if you can only 'just' afford to buy at today's prices and you wait until more completed properties come up for sale you may have missed the boat and been priced out of the market.

- ✓ Developers usually require staged payments from their buyers throughout the building process. This means that you don't have to make a large one-off payment. You can save for each payment, you can budget to afford each payment and you are effectively securing a high value asset for a very low initial capital outlay.

✓ Some investors buy property off-plan never intending to pay for it and certainly never intending to live in it! They take full advantage of the staged payment method and never make the final payment which is usually the largest. Instead, they put the property back onto the market just as it is about to be completed and gain profit from the natural increase in value the property has achieved throughout the period it took to build it. Obviously, this is a rather risky approach as the property market goes down as well as up and there may not be a buyer waiting in the wings at just the right moment for the vendor.

✓ Some developers use private investors to fund the building of holiday accommodation by offering them guaranteed rental yields on their completed property for a fixed period of time. This creates a symbiotic relationship as the developer has inward cash flow from the property investors to fund the building and he then has a set number of properties he can let out via holiday and tour companies or even privately for a fixed period. He then takes any excess rental yield and profits. The investor is guaranteed an income and owns a property that is ideally increasing in value over and above what it cost them to buy in the first place - everybody's happy!

THE CONS OF OFF-PLAN PROPERTY INVESTMENT

✓ By buying a property from a developer off-plan you are taking a risk on the developer. What if he encounters financial difficulties during the build and never completes or doesn't build properties to a high standard? In Colombia, developers use financial entities called "Fiducias", which are the equivalent to an escrow account. These entities make undertake extensive research into the financial status of the developer and manage the funds provided by buyers during the construction period. This is a safety net for the buyer in case the developer does not carry out the project.

✓ How secure is your investment? You need to ensure you have a watertight contract drawn up and consult independent legal representation to protect your rights and money throughout the building process. If anything happens to the builder what do you actually own? Can you get your money back? What guarantees do you have? When buying off-plan and paying in installments the title deeds are not usually drawn up in your name until completion of the build - meaning that in theory, throughout the building process the builder can re-mortgage the land on which your property will stand and until he repays the lender you cannot take legal ownership of your property.

✓ You have no way of guaranteeing the quality of the property you're buying. You need to ensure you discuss your expectations with the builder and have them written into your contract. You should also inspect previous examples of his work and make sure you have legally binding guarantees that cover the structure of the building for five to ten years.

✓ If you're buying into an area where there is not a massive amount of development going on it will be very difficult to know what the area is going to look like when finished. You have to be sure the developer will secure decent access, for example. Also, you should request information about the type of projects that are permitted by authorities to be developed in the area.

✓ You will also have to wait a long time to move into your dream home. You will be paying for it for a long time before you actually benefit from it.

So, do the pros of off-plan property investment outweigh the cons? You decide...

STEP 3: MAKE AN OFFER AND NEGOTIATE THE PRICE

WHAT YOU SHOULD KNOW ABOUT ESTIMATING HOME VALUE IN COLOMBIA.

Once you have identified your project, see here for how you can estimate home value properties in order to get a good deal. This applies to anywhere you are going to buy in Colombia, so make an offer and prepare to bargain!

MAKING AN OFFER

If you have a property that is likely to fit your needs, then you'll **make an offer** to the seller. This means that you will tell the seller how much you're willing to pay for the house. You can make the offer even if you're not 100% sure you want to buy the house.

Making the offer also generally doesn't force you to commit to buying the house no matter what. Although your **real estate agent** can give you guidance about how much to offer, you already have enough information to make your own call. In the majority of cases buyers offer a bit less than the seller is asking.

If you don't want to hassle with **negotiation** and you think the house is worth it, you can simply offer the same amount the seller is asking. If you want to try to get a better deal you can offer a little less than the seller wants, or perhaps see whether the seller will make some other concession such as paying part of the **closing costs** or undertaking some repairs.

You can also offer more than the seller is asking. This is obviously unusual, but it happens in hot markets where houses move really fast. If more than one different **prospective buyer** makes offers at the same time, the seller will usually choose the highest offer. In cases like this competitive buyers will try to outbid each other to make sure they get the house.

These are the factors to consider when coming up with your offer:

- **The advice of your real estate agent.** An agent will certainly be a lot more familiar with the market and the process than you are.

- **Your budget.** You shouldn't offer more than you can afford.

- **Payment method.** When it comes to the price... **cash got the power!** There will be always a 5%, 10% or even 30% discount for paying in advance. For property under construction or off-plan projects, although prices for new apartments are firm, usually developers give **financial discounts** for buyers providing the total down payment in advance. But this is only if you have the **cash** to pay the full price. Otherwise, don't expect a large discount.

- **The home value.** We all want to avoid **paying more** than something is worth, and this is especially true when buying a house that you may want to sell someday. But you might ignore this if the property itself is more important to you than financial value. There is nothing wrong with paying more than a house is worth if you really want the house and you can afford it. Of course, even if you are willing to pay the full asking price, it usually can't hurt to offer less to try for a better deal, unless it's a hot housing market where another buyer might outbid you.

Offering more than the market value for a home you really want works best when you don't intend to re-sell the home. An overpriced home takes longer to appreciate, but if you're not selling it then what do you care?

PRICES

To get an idea of a fair price, a good starting point is to ask for the average cost per meter in the project and compare it with others of similar characteristics in the same general area.

However, be aware that sometimes a property can cost more than another in the same block because of its particular characteristics. An old house that never has been maintained will not have the same value as one that has been completely remodeled in the same neighborhood.

From what I know of construction characteristics in the US and Europe, allow me to confirm that construction quality in Colombia is to the same or even better standards. The price for a luxury apartment in a Miami condo doesn't include any finishing characteristics, for example.

So, the relationship between price and quality is well balanced compared to what foreign buyers experience back home.

In Colombia the average cost per meter for residences in good condition varies depending on several factors including location, type of construction, number of rooms, etc.

For example:

- In the coastal area a property that is right on the sea is worth more than one that is across the street from the beach.
- Larger areas cost less per square meter than smaller.
- Condo complexes with amenities such as a swimming pool, spa, gym, a children's playground, dedicated parking space, garden area, etc. will cost more per square meter.

- Quiet locations with a residential profile that are also close to shopping malls will usually cost more than one that is in the middle of a crowded street.

For off-plan projects, developers undertake their own market study to get a better understanding of their proposed asking prices and features relative to the existing competitive market. Once the above information is analyzed, consider the initial pre-construction prices. Prices offered by developer sales offices are the same as those offered by all real estate agents.

Normally, ten story apartment projects will take 15-20 months to reach completion. During this time the developer monitors sales activity and compares it with other nearby or similar projects.

A developer will raise prices gradually during the project construction period. The increasing price rate will vary depending on market conditions. If it is a hot market the price could increase many times during the construction phase at high rates.

If prices do not increase, or if developers offer "too-good-to-be-true" special deals to buyers, this is a strong indicator of an overpriced project.

Making an offer and negotiating the price is another favorable way to estimate your home's value. Now you're ready to close the deal.

HOW DO APPRAISALS WORK IN COLOMBIA?

A real estate appraisal helps to establish a property's market value – the likely sales price it would achieve if offered in an open and competitive real estate market.

In Colombia it is common for the value of the cadastral valuation (the one used by the government for tax estimations) to be lower than commercial one (the price of a property for a commercial transaction).

This happens because the housing market has a much more dynamic flow than the information managed by government agencies.

What is the difference between commercial and cadastral valuation?

COMMERCIAL APPRAISAL

A commercial appraisal is undertaken by an accredited professional who is hired by a person, company or bank to determine the real value of a property at any given time according to their physical and topographical characteristics, in addition to environment variables that may positively or negatively affect transaction price of the property.

Typically, these appraisals are valid for only 6-12 months, as the actual prices of properties vary over time.

Banks will require an appraisal when you ask to use a home or other real estate as security for a loan because they want to make sure that the property will sell for at least the amount of money they are lending.

Don't confuse a comparative market analysis, or CMA, with an appraisal. Real estate agents use CMAs to help home sellers determine a realistic asking price. Experienced agents often come very close to an appraisal price with their CMA, but an appraiser's report is much more detailed and is the only valuation report a bank will consider when deciding whether or not to lend the money.

The appraiser is trained in analyzing the property and its surrounding local market to come up with the estimated value. A common misconception is that appraisers create value, but in reality, they interpret the market to estimate a value. They will consider things like the size of the property, its location, the amenities and the condition of the structure, to name just a few.

A professional report must contain at least the physical description of the building, an urban analysis of the area, the application of at least two methods of calculation and depending on property type, memory calculations, the photographic record, the value of appraisal and an estimate of recovery.

Minimum content

A final report made by an appraiser must contain at least the following elements:

- Property features
- Legal and land titling
- Data urban sector
- Description of services and infrastructure
- Internal characteristics, uses and location
- Memories of the calculations if needed
- Estimated recovery
- Commercial valuation (value of the property)
- Photographic record of the visit
- Attachment of documents consulted (decrees, law of reference)

At BuyColombiaRealty.com we have in-house professional appraisers if you wish to opt for this service.

CADASTRAL APPRAISAL

The cadastral appraisal determines the value of the property via through research and statistical analysis of the housing market. This type of appraisal is made by the government in each municipality. The head institute in Colombia is called the "Instituto Geografico Agustin Codazzi".

The cadastral value of each property is calculated by adding together the partial appraisals that are performed independently for the land and the buildings within it.

It is very common in Colombia for the seller and buyer to agree to register the sale for a lower value in order to save **closing costs** and also for tax purposes. This is not illegal; however, you have to bear in mind whether there is a real benefit in the long term. You must also keep in mind that if you accept this alternative, the sales value may not be less than the cadastral value for that fiscal year.

STEPS TO CONSULT CADASTRAL APPRAISALS FOR PROPERTIES IN BOGOTA ON THE INTERNET

Since 2008 the Cadastral District office of Bogota has been updating property information around the city.

As a result of this process, information will be updated for the physical, legal and economic use of urban land in the city.

1 – Go to http://www.catastrobogota.gov.co (information only available in Spanish).

2 – Check-in to the portal as a user by typing in your personal data. (If you are a registered user, just type in your username and password)

3 - Record the properties that are in your name. This allows you to keep track of the details of your property. (Note that only the owner can perform this procedure)

4 - To check the cadastral value of properties other than your own, click on the "Consulta Avaluo" - Appraisal Consultation - menu in the left column.

5 - Enter any of the following information for the properties you want to see:

- Address

- Cadastral Number

- CHIP

- "Matricula Inmobiliaria" real estate registration number

6 - Check the appraisal. In this step, the system generates a PDF file containing the respective certification of appraisal that can be downloaded directly onto your computer or a portable storage device.

STEP 4: DEFINE YOUR PAYMENT METHOD

HOW TO PAY FOR YOUR REAL ESTATE PROPERTY IN COLOMBIA

What is the best way to pay? It depends entirely on the individual.

You can bring money to Colombia and withdraw if you want – but make sure to do it right the first time.

You also have these alternatives:

1. Commercial real estate loans in your home country.

Interest rates are low in your home country. So, why don't you use that in your favor?

Some banks and other financial institutions are promoting credit loans for Colombian non-residents. This is because there are a lot of Colombians living abroad who send back what they earn to their relatives in Colombia and most of this money is used to buy or repair real estate.

If you have a Colombian partner, you can apply for this kind of credit loan. There are several companies that

110

act as mortgage brokers. Yes, there is a lot of paperwork that has to be done in the foreign country. But it is a good option for a **Colombian non-resident** and their foreign partner if they are legally established abroad.

And what about you, the Foreigner?

In most developed countries, interest rates are at an all-time low. Many people with limited funds are taking advantage of low interest rates by borrowing against the built-up equity they may have in their homes. **Commercial Loans** are being offered at rates of 3% and lower.

To avoid complications and keep it simple, get a loan in your **home country.** If you have the capacity to repay these loans even if you lose your job or have a major illness, this can be a great way to use your net worth by investing in bargain priced property in **prime Colombian locations**.

2. International Money Transfer.

You can wire the funds from your personal bank to the seller's account. Be sure to register properly in Colombia. We cover more in detail later in this chapter.

3. Mortgage Loans in Colombia.

Mortgage loans are only for Colombian citizens and their foreign spouse.

Mortgage **loan rates** for real estate in Colombia have fluctuated over the last five years between nine to twelve percent annually, depending on the economic environment. Fortunately, Colombia is known for rigorous economic management that keeps interest rates steady. These types of loans are short term, usually five to fifteen years (up to twenty percent for leasing contracts) and are primarily given to **Colombian nationals**. In most of the cases there is no seller financing. The way mortgages work in Colombia is detailed in the next chapter.

4. Cash or checks.

When buying property abroad you stand more chance of winning the property if you are willing to make payment via hard currency. If you are interested in paying cash, you are likely to be offered an agreeable discount or upgrade, thereby sealing the deal faster.

The negotiating power of cash (i.e., a wire transfer via traditional banks) can help buyers obtain a lower price or a faster closing.

However, if you frequently travel in and out to Colombia, you can use also use literal cash. It is completely legal, but also not the safest method.

Colombian law allows people the input or output of money up to USD10,000 (or its equivalent in other currencies) without being obliged to declare it to customs officials.

An amount exceeding USD 10,000 can only take place via authorized secure transportation companies.

Checks in foreign currencies in an amount above the aforementioned value must be declared at customs in Colombia. These checks cannot be deposited in Colombian accounts. Management of these is costly and often delayed.

For purposes of safety, time, cost and exchange regulation making payments in cash, checks in a foreign currency or a credit card are simply are not the best alternative.

5. Retirement Accounts – The Self-Directed LLC.

Millions of Americans already have an Individual Retirement Account (IRA). Chances are you're probably one of them.

But many people don't fully understand how an IRA works. They know that there are some tax benefits associated with it, but most people open one because someone told them they should, without fully understanding the potential of an IRA.

One of the more exciting aspects of purchasing real estate in your retirement plan is that you can buy virtually any type of property.

6. Home Country Financing.

One of the easiest ways to borrow money for the purchase of property in another country can be to take out a Home Equity Line of Credit (HELOC) on a property in the United States. This offers a couple of advantages.

If you are European looking to take advantage of cheap debt, remember that long-term fixed-rate mortgages are more common in some countries than others. Every market is slightly different, but Germany and France have longer fixed-rate terms than Spain and the U.K., for example. A 20-year mortgage can be had in Paris or Frankfurt at a rate of less than one percent.

HOW DO YOU DEAL WITH MORTGAGE CREDITS IN COLOMBIA?

The first thing someone in Colombia must consider when thinking about getting a mortgage loan is how much they can afford to pay based on their family income.

By law, a financial entity can provide up to 70% of the value of the property. The remaining 30% or down payment must be paid in cash.

For new housing you can make the down payment over the pre-construction period (about 6 to 24 months).

MORTGAGE CREDIT SYSTEMS

Credit in Pesos:

The installments remain fixed throughout the term of the loan and are based on annual rates which fluctuate between 16 and 22%. There are additions to capital from the first installment. The debt declines after the first payment.

The user knows the value of each and every one of the installments of credit and has certainty that it will never vary.

These are the options in Pesos:

Fixed amortization to Capital in pesos. The installments are slightly higher at the beginning of the credit life, but then begin to decline. This is the reason it is the cheapest option.

As installments are higher at the beginning, you will need to have a high monthly income in order to apply. Other systems require a lower monthly income.

Fixed fee in pesos. Installments are the same from beginning to end. However, the contribution to capital gradually makes it a little more expensive due to the effect of interest rates. (The cost is very similar to the average installment in UVR, as discussed below).

Credit in Unidad de Valor Real (UVR):

The UVR is a daily account unit set by the Central Bank of Colombia (Banco de la República) according to the variation in the Consumer Price Index of Colombia. The value of UVR is expressed in terms of Colombian Pesos per UVR. It is used to denominate and update mortgage loans and some public debt bonds.

If inflation is stable your installments are fixed, but if it fluctuates up or down, the same happens to the value of the payments.

The UVR is now settled on a projected inflation rate ranging between four and five percent a year. (Comment update: Banco de la República is bound by constitutional mandate to keep the inflation rate within a one-digit margin, and since 2005 has had an average low of 5%. Despite the 2020 worldwide pandemic, inflation rate in Colombia was 1.61% ending 2020, the lowest in the last ten years.

There are several options within the UVR option:

Fixed installment in UVR (lower installment value): The value of the installment increases every month in line with inflation and never decreases.

Fixed amortization to capital in UVR (average installment value): This system is more economical because after half the timeline of the loan has passed the installment value declines. However, banks do require more income capacity and paperwork to apply.

Cycle UVR system (stable annual installments): In this system the quotas never diminish. Installments increase every year according to the annual rate of inflation.

MORTGAGE CREDIT FAQS

1. How much can a bank lend?

This depends on the family income (wife and husband), or the total income for a single person.

Essentially, they determine that the value of the installment you can afford represents approximately 30% of your income.

Many banks have online simulators so you can calculate in advance the value of your installment and the amount you can borrow.

2. How much can the value of the installments be?

That depends on the terms of the loan and the conditions agreed with the bank. In the case of housing subsidized by the government (VIS), the rate is four to five base points lower.

Long term interest rates have remained stable over the last five years, so on average you could calculate approximately $14.000 pesos per million credit value. For example, for 50 million pesos worth of credit, the first installment would be around $750.000.

3. What is the timeframe of the loan?

While each bank offers different options, deadlines typically range between five and fifteen years.

4. What is the total cost of a credit loan?

This is difficult to determine accurately because interest fluctuates daily and credit conditions vary. However, you can use banks websites calculators to get an idea.

5. Will installments change during the timeframe of the credit loan?

It depends whether your credit is in pesos or UVR. If your credit is in pesos the variation is slightly lower.

In UVR installments will usually rise in value every year. One hundred pesos today is not equal to one hundred pesos tomorrow as the money loses value with the passage of time. In order not to lose or damage their liquidity, the banks convert the money lent to UVR. For this, banks multiply the credit amount by the current value of the UVR.

6. Where do I request a credit loan?

The entities legally authorized by the government to fund housing are cooperatives, employees' mutual funds, National Savings Fund (FNA), savings and housing corporations, commercial finance companies and commercial banks.

7. Is the cost of a loan the same for all banks and entities?

No. Although the law sets maximum interest rates, each financial entity decides which to apply according to market conditions. For example, cooperatives and employees' mutual funds often provide the lowest interest while banks usually charge up to the permitted limit.

You need to undertake market research to find out which bank offers the lowest rate and conditions and then decide which is best for you.

WHAT ABOUT MORTGAGE LOANS FOR FOREIGNERS?

HOW CAN FOREIGNERS OBTAIN A MORTGAGE IN COLOMBIA?

Well, there is good and bad news. First the bad…

Let's begin by noting that is not easy for foreigners to get a mortgage loan in Colombia. There are several reasons for this, but ultimately unless you are a Colombian resident, you will have a hard time getting a Colombian bank loan.

However, and this is the good news, there are certain conditions that allow foreigners to apply for financing with a local bank.

Some banks evaluate the possibility of a mortgage loan for foreigners if:

1. You are married to a Colombian national

2. You plan to buy to live-in and not as a second home

3. You have been living in Colombia for more than six months

4. You already have a local bank account

In this guide I'm going to focus on the first option, marrying a Colombian national, which is the easiest and quickest way for foreigners to obtain a mortgage loan in Colombia, and also the most common scenario for 80% of my clients.

These are the most common mortgage credit sources for Colombians and their foreign spouses living abroad:

COLOMBIAN BANKS

Initially these institutions limited their coverage to Colombians living in Miami, New York and Madrid. However, some banks have now expanded their network of services in correlation with their correspondent branch abroad. These entities examine the applicant's repayment and income capacity in their country of residence and they inspect the property in Colombia and request a local co-signer for the debt.

By law in Colombia a bank can lend up to 70% of the value of the property to be secured by a mortgage. 30% of the balance must be paid in cash.

In general, banks estimate that the value of the installment payments should be about 30% of the debtor's monthly income. If you are Colombian married to a foreigner, some banks may accept the foreign spouse's income as part of your household income.

Currently, Colombian banks only provide mortgage loans in Colombian local currency (Colombian pesos).

Some of the banks that offer mortgage credits in Colombia include:

- ScotiaBank Colpatria

- Bancolombia

- Banco Bilvao Vizcaya Argentaria (BBVA)

- Davivienda

A Colombian spouse living in the United States can apply for a mortgage credit with any Colombian bank, regardless of whether it is based in Miami, Madrid, London or New York. Make sure to ask for different credit scenarios, times of payments, cost of the credit, amount of financing).

Each bank has different application policies, and some of them accept family income (wife and husband) as a guarantee for a credit loan.

INTERNATIONAL FINANCIAL INSTITUTIONS OPERATING IN COLOMBIA

We have also worked with International companies that grant credit for Colombians and their foreign spouses living abroad. These companies provide free investment credit mortgages that are backed up by a property in Colombia. The advantage of this type of entities is that they do not depend on local variables such as inflation or interest fluctuation and do not rely on credit bureaus in Colombia such as *Central de Información Financiera CIFIN* or *Central de Información Crediticia –Datacredito-*.

How to begin?

To start your mortgage credit adventure in Colombia, bear in mind the following points:

1. Every step in the process requires legalizations, letters, signatures, documents, income statements, receipts of wire transfers to Colombia, letter sources of funds, etc.

If you want to do the process by yourself, make sure to have a minimum of 60 calendar days at your disposal between having chosen the property and the signing of the mortgage papers with the bank. If you can't be in Colombia for an extended period, it is recommended that you hire an experienced attorney, or professional real estate agent to write/review any buying/selling agreement, oversee the process as it moves through the proper legal channels and resolve all potential legal issues including loans, cancellation of pre-existing trusts, tax appraisals, notary requirements, etc. This must be made through a power of attorney, legalized in a Colombian consulate in your home country. Don't worry though, it will all be undertaken in the name of the resident abroad.

2. Select the financial institution you're going to get your mortgage credit from.

According to each bank policy, a mortgage credit can be assigned for up to 70% of the housing value, in amounts that can range from 50 to 400 million pesos.

3. Select the line of credit that suits your financial capacity.

You can choose between a fixed interest rate, provided in "pesos" or a variable interest rate known as Units of Real Value (UVR), both of which have deadlines ranging from a minimum of 5 years to a maximum of 15 years. Or you can opt for a credit loan in US dollars.

4. The mortgage requires taking out life insurance and fire-earthquake insurance.

a. Life insurance: required for the amount of credit approved. If you are 55 years or older, or the value of the credit is more than COL$150,000,000 the applicant must undergo a medical examination and legalize it in their country of residence.

b. Earthquake and fire insurance: required for the commercial value of the property as collateral.

5. A mortgage credit loan generates additional costs such as:

a. Title recording study.

b. Appraisal.

c. Additional costs of deeds at the notary and registration office for the amount of the credit.

These must be paid throughout the credit loan process.

6. General documents required by foreigners to apply for a mortgage loan:

- Certificate of residence from their home country.

- Individual credit application for living abroad in a bank that offers this option (see banks listed at the end of this chapter).

- Legible photocopy of an ID card containing fingerprints and your signature.

- Original special power of attorney, if applicable, with no more than three months of signature date (legalized in the applicant's country of residence).

- Proof of the applicant having send money orders requested from within Colombia during the past six months (this can be through various banks or money exchange offices like Western Union).

- Letter to the bank or entity confirming the payment method that will be used for the payment of monthly credit loan fees.

INTERNATIONAL MONEY TRANSFERS FOR BUYING COLOMBIAN REAL ESTATE

YOU CAN ORGANISE A MONEY TRANSFER FROM YOUR PERSONAL BANK INTO THE SELLER'S ACCOUNT IN COLOMBIA. HOWEVER, BEFORE DOING ANYTHING PLEASE CHECK YOUR BANK'S POLICIES.

Local banks now have representatives all over the world. Ask your bank the time is will take to transfer the money, the name of the local partner overseas, and the ways you can track your money transfer.

In many ways, the Colombian **banking system** is very progressive.

You can work with a **Colombian bank** with no doubts. It could be the easiest, sure and fastest way.

When buying a house or apartment in off-plan projects the **developer** may have an international account and you will be able to organize a money transfer directly to the seller's **overseas account**.

In most cases you can wire the money from your bank to the developer's fiduciary account in Colombia (similar to an escrow account). This process is simplified because there is already an established relationship between the bank and the developer.

As with everything, there are exceptions to the rule, and you can have some issues in the meantime. Papers can be missed by inefficient employees. This is when a professional **real estate agent** makes a difference. It is important to have a local expert who can help you to deal with real people in the local language.

Overseas money transfers have some requirements to prevent **money laundering**, and the Colombian government is no exception.

Your home bank can confirm your credibility as an honest person with **'clean money'** because they already know you, they have your transactions records, your credit history and so on. If you have nothing to 'hide', this simple record will also help establish you in

> **IMPORTANT TIP:** *The parties (buyer and seller) may agree that money sent to buy the property can be declared via Form 5 (Formulario No. 5) as a simple wiring of money or via form 4 (Formulario No.4) as a foreign investment in Colombia.*
>
> *Using either form you can exercise your foreign exchange rights, such as remitting abroad the product of the sale and its profits when you need to resell the property. It's as simple as that!*

Colombia as a law-abiding person.

The government has made some changes to streamline the registration procedure for foreign investment. In the case of buying property, until the end of 2009 a Form

No. 11 was required by Central Bank (Banco de la República) to register your money transfer when buying real estate as a foreign investment.

This has now changed and the process occurs **automatically, when Form No. 4** is filed at the local bank that receives the money.

In case you forget to issue instructions, **banks file form No. 5 by default** (Formulario No. 5). This is okay because Colombian law guarantees the right of ownership regardless of nationality or country of residence.

So, what is the difference between forms No. 4 and 5?

With form No. 4 you receive a written guarantee by Colombian law (Decree 2080 of 2000 articles 10 and 11 and its modifications), stating that private ownership and other rights acquired may not be disavowed or breached by subsequent laws except for public utility or social interest reasons. It also gives you also the advantage of being eligible for an investors visa.

However, once you have sold the property you have to cancel the foreign investment registration by giving notice to the Central Bank (Banco de la República). See more details in section 9.1.2.

With form No. 5 you can sell the property at any time without the need to inform any authority. The advantage to this is the simplicity of the both the procedure and its eventual termination.

SENDING MONEY TO COLOMBIA IN 5 EASY STEPS

1. Always sign a Purchase Agreement. A copy of this document will support the purpose of the transaction. Including the seller's Colombian bank account number is not compulsory but it is a plus.

2. Agree in advance a fixed exchange rate with the seller, so that whatever the number of days it takes to deposit the funds in pesos into the sellers account, there are no discrepancies.

3. All transfers of money (USD/EUROS) must be done through a Colombian financial Institution

Money laundering is an issue so be prepared to submit kind of several types of documentation to the seller's bank (personal/corporate tax returns, employee letters, bank introduction letters) in order to certify that the source of the funds being transferred is legal and that the purpose of the transfer is a real estate transaction.

4. Once you make your transfer, be sure that it is registered by the bank as a Foreign Direct Investment (FDI) in Colombia. The receiving bank will fill out this form, checking box 6 - "Inmuebles". Keep a copy of each form for every transaction.

5. Local financial institutions are required to exchange all funds transferred into Colombia into United States dollars before exchanging them for Colombian Pesos. In normal international wire transfer money is in sort kind of limbo between the Foreign Bank and the local bank. The seller must ask their bank to monetize it in pesos and put into Sellers local account.

ALTERNATIVES FOR SENDING MONEY TO COLOMBIA...

Do not worry about traveler's checks or exchanging money at the airport before arriving in Colombia. It is better to take your debit card and use it at the Colombian airport to withdraw pesos instead.

Your bank automatically calculates the current exchange rate and it is cheaper than going to a currency exchange. If you can withdraw 400.000 pesos (about $180) you'll be fine. Colombian ATMs only distribute pesos, not US dollars. Find out your ATM withdrawal rates from your bank ahead of time.

If you think it will be difficult to obtain a bank account in Colombia, I have listed at nine different ways to send money to Colombia from your home bank without any problem. Some of them are instant, others require time to be activated, so take the time to study what work best for you.

NINE DIFFERENT WAYS TO SEND MONEY TO COLOMBIA:

1. Local ATMs: With the Visa, Master, Diners and American Express debit cards issued by your home bank, you can withdraw funds from most ATMs in Colombia. Be sure to account for ATM withdrawal fees that will vary from bank to bank and let your bank know that you will be using your card in Colombia so that their fraud catchers won't freeze the transaction. There are thousands of ATMs in almost every town in Colombia and although some work exclusively for specific bank customers the vast majority allow Visa and MasterCard debit cards. Check whether they have the Visa and MasterCard logos on them.

There are also recommendations for the use of Colombian ATMs. Scammers and thieves target ATM users every day, so see below for recommendations that also to foreigners:

✓ Use ATMs in places you are familiar with or where you feel comfortable, like malls, inside a bank or a secure area.

✓ If you can, don't use ATMs at night or after a big aguardiente party! It's common to run out of money when the night is good!!

✓ Avoid ATMs with signs like "En Reparacion", "En Pruebas" or any other artificial sign stating that is temporary out of order or under maintenance

✓ Although Colombians are very happy to supply information in the street, asking for help when using an ATM is not a good idea.

✓ Avoid ATMs that present difficulties when inserting your card

✓ Don't rush. Take the time you need to make the transaction and put the money in your pocket before leaving the cabin.

✓ Ask for a printed receipt. This will help you later if there are any problems with the transaction.

✓ As a general rule you can withdraw up to $800.000 pesos a day (about USD 400) at a Colombian ATM. That's almost twice the minimum monthly wage for a regular Colombian worker. But do be aware that using ATMs excessively in Colombia can result in a lot of ATM fees – sometimes up to USD$5 per use.

2. Western Union: This is the most common method in the case of an emergency and is nearly instantaneous for recipients who need money quickly. However, it can be very costly to send, particularly if you choose to send the money online (about $10 more per $100) instead of going to the local grocery store in person to send it. Recipients are also charged for receiving money, however they do have Bilingual assistance and discount cards for repeated use of service.

3. Money Gram: Similar to Western Union but they advertise lower rates. You can send money online from your checking account or e-Check from your bank account or go to a Money Gram locale to pay in cash. Using Money Gram, you can send a 10-word message to your recipient and you also get a three-minute-long distance call. There is also a "Money Saver" card for discounts for repeated use.

4. PayPal: This is the most popular payment system on the Internet, now with other value-added services. New accounts qualify for a PayPal MasterCard debit card. You can send or withdraw money anywhere, especially at the airport in Colombia when you forget to budget for the exit tax ($31 for tourists, $54 for business travelers). You can also send the card to someone in Colombia to use at ATMs while you add funds online from the U.S. Transferring money from your bank account to your PayPal account is free but can take four to five business days.

5. Payoneer: Payoneer provides online transaction services and e-commerce solutions to 200 countries worldwide, allowing professionals from all around the globe to send, receive and convert funds in more than 100 currencies. They are a worldwide service provider of MasterCard and they use the midpoint of MasterCard's official currency rates at the time of conversion.

Payoneer users may also apply for a MasterCard debit card connected to their account, which will allow them to access their funds anywhere for an annual fee of $29.99. The card is for individuals only. Payoneer offers three basic mass payment packages for businesses processing payments on a regular basis:

Plan Type	Small Business	Corporate	Enterprise
Beneficiaries required	10 or more	20 or more	200 or more
Monthly payouts	$10K or more	$80K or more	$250K or more

Source: Payoneer.com

Unlike other providers, there are no per-transaction fees for the sender. Instead, the beneficiary will be charged a fixed $3 per transfer (unless you choose to bear that cost). The funds on a Payoneer account will be instantly available on the beneficiary's Payoneer MasterCard and they can withdraw from any ATM in Colombia.

Payoneer is affordable and offers more convenient ways to access funds in Colombia, in addition to being a great way to pay your remote employees.

6. Ria: Ria is another simple way to send money internationally. The downside is the smaller list of countries from which you can send payments. The countries you can send money from are the U.S., Canada, New Zealand, Australia, Chile, and certain European countries. However, the fees are worth considering, especially when sending a payment from the U.S. to Colombia is only $5.

7. Transferwise: TransferWise makes transferring money to Colombia a breeze: it only requires the amount being sent and the destination. Then you make a local payment to TransferWise, either through a bank transfer, "swift" transfer, or debit / credit card, and the process is complete.

TransferWise converts your money at the real interbank exchange rate, saving you a lot of money (even compared to those who promise you "zero commissions"). To know whether you're getting the best possible rates when sending money online to Colombia, you'll need to know what the real exchange rate (also called the mid-market rate) is.

TransferWise offers a rate tracker tool that you can use to find the actual mid-market exchange rate at any time. You can use this information to know when a payment solution is marking up their fees, and to assist when finding the best deal possible.

8. Xoom: This is a money transfer service that offers direct service to a lot of countries including Colombia. Xoom will transfer money from your home bank account, a PayPal account, debit card or eCheck. Your recipient can pick up the money in minutes at any **Davivienda, BBVA** or" Pagos Internacionales" location. You can also make fast bank deposits to a checking or savings account in Colombia at most banks. The recipient is emailed a tracking number to check the status of the transfer. Check out their site for rates, details, participating banks and delivery restrictions. This is a well-known and long-time money transfer service so you can be certain of the services they offer.

9. Viamericas: accepts your money via telephone, online, check or money order and delivers it to your recipient via direct bank deposit, home delivery (not available in Colombia) or pickup at a Viamericas locale. Viamericas also can be used to pay for the recipient's bills for health care, utilities, mortgage and credit cards.

10. WorldRemit: WorldRemit is an easy solution for sending payments to Colombia. Their online calculation tool lets you know exactly what you can expect to pay. In addition to this, payments can be sent and received from a wide range of countries.

Compared to other tools, WorldRemit fees are one of the lowest for bank deposits.

WorldRemit costs for sending money to Colombia (2020 update):

US to Colombia $1.99 USD

Canada to Colombia $3.99 CAD

UK to Colombia   £2.99 GBP

Australia to Colombia $3.99 AUD

HOW TO OPEN A BANK ACCOUNT IN COLOMBIA IF YOU ARE A FOREIGNER

FIRST, KEEP IN MIND THAT YOU DON'T NEED A COLOMBIAN BANK ACCOUNT, A CÉDULA DE EXTRANJERÍA OR ANY TYPE OF VISA TO BUY REAL ESTATE IN COLOMBIA.

You can send a money transfer directly from your foreign bank account to the seller's account. The time the money transfer takes depends on each bank. Sometimes the money is available the same day and sometimes it can take between five and ten days. Always ask your bank and the seller's bank how long the transaction will take to avoid headaches later in the process.

However, if you don't feel comfortable sending money to the seller's account and you are planning on a longer stay in Colombia, you could consider opening one. It may not be easy as some banks require lots of documents and the back and forth interactions can take time.

REQUIREMENTS

As a general rule foreigners are not allowed to open a bank account in Colombia unless they have lived in Colombia for more than six months.

To do it you will need to have a Cédula de Extranjería - Alien Identification Card or Colombian ID for foreigners-, and to have a Cédula de Extranjería you must be a holder of a visa that has been issued for more than three months - for example, a resident, immigration or temporary visa. You will find more detailed information about this in **The Colombia Visa Guide,** other book you can have in our website buycolombiarealty.com.

It's also very important to have a personal introduction from a Colombian national. If you do not have the right introduction, 99% of the time a bank will not open an account for you even if you have the cédula de extranjería. Of the most importance to a bank manager is that the foreigner has the intention to remain in the country or at least a strong link with Colombia.

It can be easier if you are married to a Colombian native and you may be able to open a joint account with them. As with many procedures in Colombia, things works better when you have a "palanca" (advantages you might have with people you know in private or public entities) or some kind of influence. In this case some bank managers are willing to open bank accounts using only a passport. They will do it if you are well introduced to them by a local person. This is not a common rule, but it can sometimes work in this way.

THINGS TO BEAR IN MIND

a) The temporary registered number issued by Migración Colombia (known as "contraseña" or Password) is the document that certifies that the cedula is being completed and it can't be used as an ID number. The bank can reject it as it is not a complete ID that matches the requirements of the "Protocol anti-terrorism".

b) As the bank and the client have a private contract, the bank can decide whether it will accept the client and which ID or documents the person will need to show.

c) If for any reason you can't wait until you get the correct ID, you can ask the DAS if they consider the "contraseña" a suitable ID. If they do and you also have a letter of introduction, the bank may open a bank account in accordance with their internal standards.

FREQUENTLY REQUESTED DOCUMENTS

Most Colombian banks will ask you to provide at least the following documents, however, they have the right to ask for more papers if they deem it necessary:

- A letter of introduction from your personal bank at home

- Proof of income (a letter from your company and/or your bank statements) stating the source of your funds

- A photocopy of your cédula de extranjería

- In some banks the copy of a promise of purchase agreement contract is also valid

- The initial amount in pesos for an initial deposit. This varies between banks.

ADVANTAGES OF HAVING A BANK ACCOUNT

✓ Having a Colombian account allows you to pay bills (cable, phone, utilities and often your rent) online. This means that if you are frequently out of the country you can pay your bills from anywhere at any time or even automatically.

✓ If you want to transfer money from another country into Colombia, you have a safe location.

✓ It can make obtaining other things in the future a bit easier, like credit loans and credit cards.

✓ Bank statements are compulsory to get a post-paid cellphone plan.

✓ It will help you to develop a record of usage in banks databases.

✓ It contributes to a sense of belonging by linking you to a local account for business transactions.

✓ You could benefit from currency exchange fluctuations. When you send money from your home bank to a Colombian bank you only can withdraw pesos, and the bank calculates the exchange rate on the date you make the transaction. You only have to check the exchange rate on the day and transfer the funds when it's good for you.

INTERNATIONAL BANKS IN COLOMBIA

International banks own about 25% of banking assets in Colombia. After the US financial debacle, that is good news!

The following are the most important international banks with branches in Colombia. (Although, if you ask me, I wouldn't set my hands on fire for any of these!!):

Scotiabank Colombia (formerly Citibank). The Canadian Financial group Nova Scotia, known in Colombia as Scotiabank bought the entire credit consumer line of Citibank, a bank that had been established in Colombia since the 1980's. Their ATM cards can be used in any ATM in either country and there are no ATM fees for using a Scotiabank ATM in Colombia.

BBVA. A member of the Spanish multinational banking group Banco Bilvao Viscaya Argentaria. The only international bank with an introductory page in English.

Banco GNB Sudameris (Formerly HSBC). In 2012, the Colombian Group bought the commercial operations of HSBC in Colombia, Peru and Paraguay.

THE LARGEST COLOMBIAN BANKS

Three large domestic banking groups control 60% of Colombian banking assets: Aval Group, Bancolombia and Banco Davivienda. These are the most popular Colombian banks in the Colombian expatriate community:

Bancolombia. The first Colombian bank to trade its stocks at the New York Stock Exchange. They have plenty of information about the history of the bank history and events for investors in English.

Banco Davivienda. A member of the Bolivar Insurance Group, it is the third major bank of its kind in Colombia.

The AVAL group. The largest financial group in Colombia. It is comprise of four Banks: Banco de Bogotá, Banco AV Villas, Banco de Occidente and Banco Popular.

COLOMBIAN CURRENCY

The Colombian currency exchange rate has fluctuated over the last five years around $3000 to $3.800 per 1USD. Economic authorities in Colombia are working to keep the exchange rate in this range. However, recent fluctuations in the global economy and increased foreign capital inflow in sectors such as mining have weakened the dollar by lowering this value. You can check Google for the current exchange rate every time you need to make a wire transfer.

As a friend used to say, the 1,000 peso bill is great to impress your friends back home or to roll your own smokes if you're out of Marlboros. You should carry some 20,000 peso bills but mostly 10,000s and 5,000s. If you often need lots of 50,000 peso bills you should use your credit/debit card instead.

You really don't want to flash many 50,000 pesos bills around. Aside from attracting LOPM (lovers of other people's money), many vendors and particularly taxi drivers hate making change, will simply tell you, "Sorry, I don't have change", and you will end up having to go around every cigar store asking for change.

In March 2016 the Bank of the Republic issued the 100K bill (100,000 pesos). While other countries try to eliminate big denomination bills, Colombia is bucking the trend.

The Bank of the Republic board must have had their reasons, but for its critics the new hundred thousand pesos bill is a denomination too high. When comparing the value of pesos to higher bills in the US dollar or the euro, Colombian hundred thousand pesos bills are of much lower worth. Five hundred euros amounts to more than half million pesos and one hundred American dollars is currently approaching more than three hundred thousand Colombian pesos when exchanged. However, if you do manage to get a 100K bill, make sure it's not counterfeit!

STEP 5: SIGN A PURCHASE AGREEMENT

THE SALES CONTRACT OR PROMISE OF PURCHASE AGREEMENT

Once you agree upon the price you will need to create the **sales contract**. In Colombia verbal and written agreements are subject to the same enforcement, but for real estate business it is always better to obtain a written agreement to ensure the buyer's rights and because of the need of the parties to be bound by a legal document.

This is called a "Promise Purchase Agreement", in which both parties can define the terms of the negotiation so it can serve as a model for the final deed.

It must include at least:

- Buyer's and seller's I.D numbers
- Price
- Title recording
- Time and method of payment. The down payment is usually about 20 - 30% of the price agreed.
- Full description of the property, including its identification name, address, boundaries, registration number, tax identification number and, also those of the condominium, if the property is part of one, including the public

deeds by means of which the property is under such condominium regime.

- A penalty clause in case of either the buyer or the seller breaks the deal (approximately 50 - 100% of the down payment).
- It must include the specific time and date or condition that sets the date to celebrate the purchase and sale agreement. In relation to this requirement, as stated by case law, it is also necessary to indicate the Public Notary where the purchase and sale agreement public deed will be executed;
- Commission plan if a real estate agent is used

Signing a purchase agreement gives the **seller** time to bring the property up to the agreed condition and to pay past due taxes and utility bills and move out.

The **buyer** uses this time to arrange for funds, prepare a trip or name someone else to act as their representative to complete the sale.

The buyer can either sign directly or via a third-party representative. In the later case, the buyer must provide a special **power of attorney** for their representative, who must also have a proof of certifiable Colombian identification to sign the contract on the buyer's behalf.

The power of attorney needs to be signed by the buyer before a public notary unless made abroad, in which case you must go to the nearest Colombian **consulate** in your home country to legalize both the document and your signature.

A power of attorney that is signed abroad is considered **valid** if legalized by the Colombian Consulate.

STEP 6: MAKE THE CLOSING AND SIGN THE DEED

THE CLOSING PROCEDURE IN COLOMBIA

Making the closing is the proverbial "signing on the dotted line." Prepare to pay for closing costs.

Closing procedures will vary according to the buyer and seller's wishes. In some cases, the buyer and seller (as well as their real estate agents) will all attend the closing. In other cases, each party will present separately. The **closing** will take place at a notary's office. In general, the closing will be attended by all of the buyers involved and their **real estate agent**, who will have reviewed all of the components of the sale contract and will be the one to say "sign here" more times than you have ever heard in your life.

To ensure everything is ready before attending the closing, the following documentation must be delivered to the notary's office to **confirm the final deed**:

1.   **Certificate of tradition** updated no greater than 30 days prior. When buying a new home from developers they must provide this information.
2.   **Photocopy** of buyer and seller's ID.
3.   **Power of attorney** issued by the buyer, if applicable.
4.   **Purchase agreement** or sales contract.

5. **Tax free property certificate** (*Paz y Salvo Predial*) which indicates that all municipal taxes on the property have been paid.

6. **Tax free value gain property certificate** (*Paz y Salvo de Valorización*) which indicates that all taxes related to the increases in the value of the property due to improvements in the local area have been paid; generally levied by all municipalities.

7. If the property is subject to a **condominium regime** (this may be the case for condos or houses in a residential complex) a payment certificate noting that all maintenance and other fees are up to date is required. Alternatively, the seller may submit a notarized copy of the public deed that contains the condominium or association rules governing the property.

8. For used properties, the effective document comprising the **deed** of the property.

Do you think this is enough paperwork? Don't worry, if you have done things properly from the beginning, these papers will have been acquired throughout.

Besides, you already have a professional **bilingual** real estate agent by your side. Right?

So, you only need to worry about arranging the trip to coming to sign.

The notary office takes one to two business days to prepare the deed. After this time, the document is ready to be signed and you have time to collect closing costs.

The notary's office gives both parties about eight to ten business days to sign the deed.

Be sure that your name and I.D is correctly written before you sign it. Any mistake in the deed will give require making a correction which will mean coming back to the notary's office and signing again.

At the **Notary's office**:

- Both the seller and buyer sign and finger print.
- The buyer must be ready to pay the seller the balance of the sales price. Normally the buyer has already paid the seller the total amount before meeting at the notary's office, via a money transfer, cashier's check drawn from a Colombian bank or in cash.
- The seller pays for and presents to the Notary, the proper amount of sales tax .
- The buyer pays the notary's fees agreed in the purchase agreement.

Within a maximum time limit of 48 hours the notary's office will send off three copies of the deed. One of these is for the legal registration at the Government's Registry Office.

CLOSING COSTS AND RELATED FEES

You need to reserve some extra money for closing costs and related fees. They are about 2 - 2.5% of the agreed upon sales price.

CLOSING COSTS INCLUDE:

- ✓ Notary expenses. These are 0.5% upon the deal value (this includes notary's fees, authentic copies, IVA sales tax, etc.).
- ✓ Registering fees (0, 5%).
- ✓ Local taxes and other charges (1%). This includes municipality taxes (*Boleta Fiscal*).
- ✓ Income Tax (paid only by the seller at 1%).

These costs are usually split between both parties unless agreed otherwise.

The following outlines the costs normally assumed by each party:

THE BUYER

- ✓ Title enquiry

- ✓ Appraisal, if needed

- ✓ Notary's office fees as agreed

✓ Registers fees as agreed

✓ Mortgage costs. If you are buying using a mortgage loan, notary and registering fees must be paid and are calculated according to the amount of the mortgage.

THE SELLER

✓ Tax free property certificate (*Paz y Salvo Predial*) which indicates that all municipal taxes on the property have been paid.

✓ Tax free value property certificate (*Paz y Salvo de Valorización*) which indicates that all taxes related to the increases in the value of the property due to improvements to the property or area have been paid.

✓ Notary's office fees as agreed

✓ If the seller is an individual, then **1% of the sales price** is deducted as withholding tax (*Retención en la fuente*).
It is deducted at the source with the objective that the income does not leave the country without being taxed.

STEP 7: PREPARE TO RECEIVE YOUR PROPERTY

Today is the big day! You will meet with the seller or the real estate advisor and complete the transaction. They will then hand over to you the property you just bought. To make sure that everything goes smoothly until the end, you need to review every detail. By now you should have a list of all the items concerning your purchase. Check this carefully, item by item.

Whether new or used, for rent or to own, there are several aspects you need to carefully consider at the time you receive the property. This will prevent unpleasant surprises from popping up after you have made the purchase.

It is important to verify that it is in accordance with the conditions specified in the agreement. Here is what to look at in detail and what not to miss.

The official delivery of a property should be done with a checklist in hand. It is the moment in which you have the opportunity to make it clear if you are satisfied or not before you sign the delivery certificate. Make absolutely sure that you have this checklist and that you go through every single detail of the property before you proceed.

Check that utilities (water, electricity, natural gas, etc.) have all been installed correctly and function properly. If the property is delivered with some appliances, you must thoroughly check the condition of each one. For example, make sure that the stove's knobs and burners work properly, and that the odor extractor and the water heater turn on without any inconvenience, among others.

Inspect the status of the paint and note the level of humidity. Be very meticulous with this and accurately record the state of the property in a written clause. Paint can deteriorate quickly under harsh conditions or if the job was done haphazardly. This could escalate into an expensive issue in the future and so you need to be very detailed in recording this. , Once the sale is consummated, both parties tend to take the agreement for granted. After the deed is signed, you might not be able to claim recompense if there is no record of your concern and everything is within the conditions agreed to by both parties.

BASIC CHECKLIST

The following list may seem obvious to some and even unnecessary for others. But in my experience, it is always a good idea to review the following:

1. Doors and windows align and work properly.

2. There is adequate ventilation and the minimum requirements are met for gas appliances if these are present or will be installed.

3. Check the condition of the carpet, floors, or tile veneer. One tip is to tap gently to verify that they are not hollow.

4. Confirm that the floor is level. For wooden floors, check that it does not produce excessive noise when you walk on it.

5. Check the water pressure, gas supply, electrical installations, and the ease of connections for telecommunications services (television, telephone, and internet).

6. Verify that the taps, toilets, and drains work properly. Similarly, check electrical sockets and switches, as well.

7. Check the condition of the paint and details that you have requested. There should be no cracks or moisture.

8. The home or property must be clean and ready to be lived in. Do not receive it if there is construction material or dirt still present in the home.

9. Of course, you are free to measure the dimensions of the rooms, and different places in the house. It's your space!

10. If you find any type of defect, report it and make sure it is in writing.

11. If the property is located within a residential complex, ask about the operation of the common areas, recreation and leisure areas, security, etc.

For New Constructions

If it is a new home, the construction company is obliged to deliver an inventory of its condition and if there is any damage, the builder must honor a one-year warranty period and make the necessary repairs and improvements. Demand that a delivery certificate be drawn up, in which all your observations on the state in which you receive the property are recorded.

Request for the documents that contain the specific conditions of the guarantees on accessories (eg: ovens, extractor hoods, heaters, among others) offered by the manufacturers of the goods and that these were installed in the property.

Also ask for the Instruction Manual on the use and installation of these accessories.

Request for the Certificates of Conformity for electrical installations according to the RETIE (Reglamento Técnico de Instalaciones Eléctricas) –Technical Guidebook for Electric Installations). If there are gas lines, demand the certificate of their correct installation.

HORIZONTAL PROPERTY REGULATION, equivalent to HOA (Home Owners Association) terms and rules

In "horizontal property" (the term used to refer to most apartment buildings in Colombia, and in general all housing complexes or communities of more than 2 units):

An essential aspect that often goes unnoticed by buyers in residential complexes is the administration, the budget, and the maintenance of the common areas.

In the case of buying in a horizontal property, the minutes of the previous HOA meeting must be requested. This is so you can analyze what happened in the preceding period and what future projects or improvements are planned for the common areas.

Another aspect, which also has to do with administration, is the quality and quantity of the residential budget. Knowing it will allow you to have savings during the first years without extraordinary fees.

You should check the amenities of the complex and areas such as the swimming pool. These generally cover a large part of the total budget and if they need to be repaired because of cracks or major damage, you will have to invest more money to cover these additional expenses.

To review all these details, you do not need the help of "experts", whether it would be your architect or engineer relative or your lawyer. They will always find more flaws than there really are. Ironically, even if they did not invest a single penny in the property, they are generally able to completely discourage you from your new purchase.

Of course it's always best to have the help of someone knowledgeable about these issues. But my point is that you can use common sense to perform the inspection. Whatever faults in the property you may find will be based on your own two eyes, and not on the opinion of experts. Sometimes the "experts" tend to criticize the work of other people. They always have something to say about the way a space is used, or they may think that the materials should be of better quality. In the end, as the owner, it is your opinion that should prevail. What others have to say should not count more than what you prefer.

But do keep an open mind. It is also very true that others can help you detect details that may not be so obvious to you.

When you buy a house subject to the horizontal property regime, you not only acquire a private property, you also have the right to common property. Find out what is included in the project (communal room, swimming pool, gym, reception, green areas, deposits, parking lots, etc.) and what characteristics such as dimensions, qualities, times and delivery times they have.

Identify which furniture, equipment and accessories are included in the commercial offer and which are only part of the decoration. It is advisable to request a listing from the developer where this information is more complete and technical completer and more technical, since generally, the demonstrators' sales agents in the salerooms do not reach that level of specificity may not know all the pertinent details and this can lead to misunderstandings at the time of purchase. This list will also be very useful at the time of delivery of the property.

Check what type of parking they offer, if it is individual or bonded, covered or not, as well as its dimensions and location within the project. Keep in mind that there are projects with communal, common parking spaces for exclusive use, or private, in accordance with the horizontal property regulations.

Find out about the construction system, the class of materials used, the availability of basic public services, the socioeconomic stratum of the project, among others.

Documents, costs and payments of your new home

Without differentiating if it is a new or used property, it is necessary to check that everything is in order. At the time of delivery, also ask for:

• Copy of Legal ownership documents, such deeds and Homeowners association's rules and regulations;

• Payment of ordinary and extraordinary administration fees without outstanding issues;

• Property tax bill, already paid;

• Public services fees without arrears;

Now that you know everything that you should review and consider when receiving your new home, don't worry about being meticulous. Ask questions, write down what needs to be improved, take an inventory, and make sure everything is clear.

Some legal considerations:

When buying a new development, sometimes advertising flyers states two different terms: Private and built area. Let's take a look at this both terms.

According to the *Superintendencia de Sociedades* (the government agency that regulates construction and real estate industry), defines:

Built Area: This area will include all the square meters that are within the perimeter of the home, including areas of dividing walls and façade, ducts, and structure (columns or structural walls). If walls are shared with a neighbor, the perimeter will be measured from the middle of the dividing wall:

Private Area: The private built area of the property excludes those walls or elements that are considered common good, such as ducts, facades, columns and structural walls that are located within the boundary of the property.

So, what is the difference between private area and built area?

Finally it is very simple: what you are buying is the **private area**. That is the area that you can modify according to your tastes and needs. This is the living area, where you can move, and the walls that if you wanted you could tear down.

On the other hand, the **built area** includes everything that is in your apartment, and not everything belongs to you because it is part of the joint ownership. It can include, machine rooms, elevator cages that may be within the perimeter of your property but that you cannot modify since they do not belong to you. In addition, it must be taken into account that the built area, as its name indicates, is the area with construction, or for better understanding, it's everything that has a roof. In the same means, terraces would not enter the built area, and they are indicated separately.

For all business practices in real estate, built area is what you will always refer to.

> **REMEMBER:** *Private area is always less than the built area.*

Consumer protection rights

In accordance with the provisions of the Consumer Statute (Law 1480 of 2011), suppliers and producers must provide consumers with clear, truthful, sufficient, timely, verifiable, understandable, accurate and suitable information on the products they offer.

It is the builders and developers who must provide all the information of their suppliers and contractors, and assume the commitment of the guarantees on the products they use.

For real estate, the legal guarantee includes the stability of the work for ten (10) years, and for finishes, one (1) year.

The parts, supplies, accessories or components attached to the real estate that must be changed for warranty effectiveness. These may not necessarily be identical to those originally installed, but should be of equal or better quality.

AT THE TIME OF RECEIVING THE HOUSING:

Verify that the areas, characteristics, and qualities correspond to those agreed in the negotiation.

Remember that the parts, supplies, accessories, or components attached to the real estate that must be changed for the effectiveness of the guarantee, may not necessarily be identical to those originally installed, but should be of equal or better quality,

Be attentive to the process of delivery and receipt of your property, as well as the completion of the Delivery Certificate, which you will have to sign to your satisfaction.

Remember that some defects usually appear with the normal use of the property. It is therefore important to find out about the type and conditions of the after-sales service that they are offering you.

Request delivery of the "User Manual", a document in which you will find valuable information regarding suppliers, materials used, plans (hydraulic and electrical) that may be useful in the future.

STEP 8: REGISTER THE OWNERSHIP OF THE PROPERTY

WHAT IS A TITLE RECORD?

A title record is a way to track the chronological chain of the property's ownership. So, one of the most important things to do before buying real estate is to check the **title records** to ensure that the property actually belongs to the person selling it and that it is not subject to any liens or other financial attachments. You can follow the chain of sales and **transfers** of the property from the original grant of the land all the way to the current owner. This is called a **title search** (*Estudio de titulos*).

This is a procedure to undertake before signing the purchase agreement. In fact, a purchase agreement must contain a clause outlining the property's previous ownership.

When using a mortgage loan, the bank will create this for you using their own legal staff.

In other scenarios you should have an experienced professional assist you to make the verification.

The first step in this process requires the seller to provide the property's ownership history and a no-lien **certificate** (Certificado de tradición y libertad), which should date back no more than one month. This will include the property's real estate registration number, owner's name and the property's **record summary**.

The certificate costs approximately US$5.

Requests for the ownership history and the **no-lien** certificate for the property can be made at the local government's records office (*Oficina de Registro de Instrumentos Públicos*) in the area where the property is located.

In addition to this the clearance of all taxes can be confirmed by obtaining an **account statement** for the property from the treasury office (*Oficina de Catastro*) of the city or district where the property is located.

After checking the title record, there are two possible scenarios:

1. If there are **no liens** against the title, the sale can proceed.

2. If there are **liens** against the title:

- The seller can commit to cleaning up the property's liens before you sign the purchase agreement.

- You can settle a clause in the purchase agreement with a time limit **committing** the seller to clear the liens associated with the property. Then an initial down payment of 20-30% of the sale price is used by the seller to **clear the liens** and other charges such as unpaid municipal taxes, public utilities, etc.

HOW DO I ORGANIZE THE RECORDING OF THE TITLE?

When you get the deed from the notary's office, you should record it at the local government's records office in the city where the property is located. The purpose of recording the deed is to give **"notice to the world"** that you now have an **ownership** interest in that particular piece of real estate property.

So, you need to register your deed before the Registry Office of Public Instruments. There, you will need to pay city and state taxes (*Boleta fiscal*). You did leave some extra money for this, right?

> **REMEMBER:** *Once issued the deed, you have two months to record your legal validity with the Government's Registry office*

The title will be recorded in the name of the buyer at the government's records office. This could take up to a week or five business days.

At this time the buyer can claim the documents showing that title has been legally **transferred** to the buyer.

After the deed is released by the Registry Office, we recommended asking for another updated **title certificate** (the one that cost US$5) to confirm that the process was undertaken properly and that the property is finally registered in your name.

We had a case in which the owner realized 20 years after buying the home that the recording was made **incorrectly** and that the property was registered in someone else's name! They had never asked for a title certificate, because they didn't need it before. Keep this in mind!

HOW TO REQUEST A TITLE CERTIFICATE ONLINE

Property owners, buyers and investors of Bogotá, Barranquilla, Medellin, Cali, Bucaramanga, Cartagena, Santa Marta and other cities will have online access to the history of any property for which they have a registration number.

This is great news because it saves time and money and you can avoid going to the offices and their unbearably long queues. In theory, if you are in **New York** and you have a house in **Bucaramanga** you can request the title certificate online while paying the same $12,000 pesos you would pay at the local Register's offices.

However, government webmasters forgot two simple internet rules: globalization and credit card payments!

The payment system is only available via local banks. So, if you are a foreigner or a Colombian living abroad, you can't use the system unless you have registered an online savings or checking account with a Colombian bank.

Things to bear in mind before trying to issue your title certificate online:

- Verify that the property is located in one of the cities and municipalities where the system is available.

List of the cities where you can get your online certificate:

Bogotá, Medellín, Cali, Barranquilla, Leticia, Cartagena, Tunja, Manizales, Florencia, Popayán, Valledupar, Montería, Quibdó, Inírida, San José del Guaviare, Neiva, Santa Marta, Villavicencio, Pasto, Cúcuta, Armenia, Pereira, San Andrés, Bucaramanga, Sincelejo, Ibagué, Puerto Carreño, Andes, Caucasia, Dabeiba, La Ceja, Sonsón, Santa Rosa de Osos, Santo Domingo, Segovia, Sitionuevo, Carmen de Bolívar, Simití, Garagoa, Moniquirá, Santa Rosa de Viterbo, Soatá, Puerto Boyacá, Anserma, Guapi, Bolívar, Caloto, El Bordo,

Puerto Tejada, Silvia, Orocué, Paz de Ariporo, Aguachica, Chimichagua, Cereté, Lorica, Sahagún, Chinú, Agua de Dios, Guaduas, La Mesa, Pacho La Palma, San Juan del Cesar, La Plata, Fundación, Plato, El Banco, Acacías, Puerto López, Barbacoas, Samaniego, La Cruz, Chinácota, Convención, Salazar de las Palmas, Puerto Asís, Piedecuesta, Puente Nacional, Málaga, San Vicente del Chucurí, Contratación, Corozal, San Marcos, Sincé, Armero, Cajamarca, El Espinal, Fresno, Guamo, Honda, Purificación, Líbano, Buenaventura y Sevilla.

- You must know the registration number or Matrícula Inmobiliaria of the properties you need titles for.
- You must have a checking or savings account in a financial institution which is registered with the ACH network and the corresponding password for internet transactions.
- You can request between one and ten online certificates per transaction in each available city.
- Check your browser, as sometimes the webpage works better with Explorer or Chrome.

STEPS TO GENERATE YOUR CERTIFICATE ONLINE

1.   Visit the webpage of the Super intendencia de   Notariado   y   registro: www.supernotariado.gov.co.

2.   Click on the button labelled "**Comprar Certificado"** which you will see flashing at the bottom right of the page.

3.   Fill in the information about the person who is buying the certificate. The platform only displays Colombian citizens ID options, but don't worry. By this point, you should already have a friend, girlfriend, wife or husband in Colombia who can help you with this.

4.   Choose the Colombian city on the list.

5.   Write the registration number of the property ("**Matricula Inmobiliaria**").

6.   Make the payment (the most frequently used credit cards are available).

7. You will receive a confirmation of the transaction with a code number that you will use to download your certificate. Be sure to print the transaction bill.

8. Choose from the left menu, the option **"Generar Certificado"** (Generate certificate).

9. A PDF file will be generated and you will also receive an email containing the PDF file. You can save the file to your PC hard drive by selecting the "Save As" button in the Adobe toolbar or you can also print it on paper.

STEP 9: REGISTER YOUR PROPERTY AS A FOREIGN INVESTMENT

THINGS YOU SHOULD KNOW ABOUT COLOMBIAN REAL ESTATE LAW

Real estate law in Colombia has undergone significant advances in the ruling of legal matters to promote housing development and to **protect** the owner's rights.

Private property is protected by Article 58 of the Colombian Constitution. According to the foregoing, *"Private property and the other rights acquired in accordance with civil laws may not be ignored or infringed upon by subsequent laws (...) expropriation will be possible pursuant to a judicial determination and with prior indemnification"*.

We have developed a stable housing legal framework because in general the government has recognized the importance of the construction and housing industry to the country's economy.

Real estate in Colombia is primarily governed by:

(i) The Colombian Civil Code which regulates the acquisition, sale and lease of properties

(ii) Law 820 of 2003, which regulates residential lease agreements

(ii) Law 675 of 2001 which regulates buildings and their use (condominiums, offices and malls) and rules on matters regarding Home Owners Associations

However, there are a number of aspects that should be considered especially by foreigners who want to invest in real estate in Colombia.

Even a foreigner won't need to hire a lawyer every time they buy a property in Colombia, but if there are other considerations involved and you want to be sure that it's done right from the beginning, feel free to hire an attorney.

Having been in this business for more than 25 years, we work with in-house lawyers who have specific experience in real estate matters.

COLOMBIAN FOREIGN INVESTMENT LAW

Throughout the last decade Colombia has made considerable progress regarding its foreign investment legislation. Thanks to this progress these procedures are now much faster and less uncertain for investors.

According to the World Bank's "Doing Business Report", Colombia is ranked 1st in Latin America and 10th in the world in the Investor Protection index. We take a lot of pride in reassuring investors that the rules governing their investment are not to be arbitrarily changed and that there is no discrimination between local and foreign investors, hence the legally embedded principles of equal treatment and stability.

There are no limits to investing in Colombia and it does not require prior governmental authorization. However, each investment must be registered with Colombia's Central Bank so that foreign investors can secure their foreign investment rights, which solidifies their right to repatriate an investment.

Existing foreign investment law in Colombia has given full legal rights to foreign citizens who want to invest in Colombian real estate.

As a foreign citizen you can **buy** and **own** real estate in a safe and confident manner.

It used to require a lot of paperwork, but it is now much easier for foreign citizens to buy real estate in Colombia!

Colombia Law benefits **international real estate investment** by:

Allowing foreigners to buy, own, record, sell or rent real estate without limitation and return the sale proceeds to their country of **origin**.

Eliminating former documents required to act as a permanent business person.

Repealing a **constitutional** provision that empowered the Colombian government to confiscate foreign-owned property without providing any compensation.

Stability. Investment reimbursement and profit remittance conditions that come into force on the date on which investments are registered may not be modified in any way that may be detrimental to the investor.

Protecting Ownership rights. Private ownership and other rights acquired may not be disavowed or breached by subsequent laws except for public utility or social interest reasons. In any case, expropriation for public utility or for social interest reasons is guaranteed to be conducted through a proper process and with adequate indemnification. You have the same rights as if you were a Colombian Citizen!

WHO IS A FOREIGN INVESTOR?

A foreign investor is understood to be any individual not residing in Colombia and any foreign corporation investing resources from abroad.

It is presumed that a person depicted as a foreign investor in the various forms used for registration with Banco de la República (Colombian Central Bank) is a non-resident. Nevertheless, all such persons must keep the documents evidencing their nonresident status.

For the Colombian foreign exchange regime, loans and operations implying foreign indebtedness do not constitute foreign investment.

The previous law required foreign citizens to have a local foreign ID (Cedula de extranjeria) or have someone with a Cedula to act as their official agent, when signing the deed.

Now you do not need a cedula or visa, just your **passport** with a valid Tourist 60 or 90 day stamp. The notary will ask you for this at the moment of signing the deed (*Escritura*).

TYPES OF FOREIGN INVESTMENT

Colombian legislation addresses two types of foreign investment: direct foreign investment and portfolio investment.

Acquiring real estate, stock certificates in real estate securitization processes or real estate funds, is considered a **direct foreign investment**.

INVESTMENT METHODS

In Colombia, foreign investment may be made via various methods:

- In cash, by importing foreign currency to be converted to local currency, used to invest directly into a company's corporate capital.

- In kind, through either tangible or intangible assets.

- By capitalizing resources in local currency that has a right to be drawn abroad.

FOREIGN INVESTMENT REGISTRATION

All foreign investments, regardless of their type or method, should be registered at the Banco de la República (Central Bank) as a condition that allows the foreign investor to exercise the foreign exchange rights conferred thereto by the law.

Once the investment is registered, the investor has the following foreign exchange rights:

✓ Remitting capital abroad and proven net profits periodically generated by his investments, i.e. the rent of a property.

✓ Reinvesting the profits or retaining as surplus any undistributed profits with drawing rights.

✓ Capitalizing any amounts bearing drawing rights, generated by investment-related obligations.

✓ Remitting abroad any amounts obtained from selling the investment in Colombia, or from liquidating the company or its portfolio, or from a capital reduction, i.e. the surplus in the sale of the property.

FOREIGN EXCHANGE DECLARATION

Every investment made by a foreigner, including foreign exchange entering the country through persons who are not Colombian residents, that is intended as a capital contribution for a company or a branch of a foreign corporation, must be registered as a foreign investment with the Bank of the Republic.

It must be registered by the person who is performing the operation, their representative or special agents (not necessarily an attorney).

The registration is automatic and forms are submitted to the Central Bank via the exchange market intermediaries (the Colombian banks who receive the money).

This procedure can be undertaken with Form 4 and Form 11. Using both forms, you, as a buyer of a property in Colombia can sell it whenever you want and transfer the money abroad.

Although banks in Colombia must provide the forms, you can get an updated version or book a consultation at the central bank's website.

CANCELLATION OF FOREIGN INVESTMENT & REGISTRATION OF REAL ESTATE IN THE SALE OF A PROPERTY

In cases involving the sale of the investment to **Colombian nationals or** a **foreign investor** (for our purposes the sale of real estate property) in part or total, the seller is responsible for obtaining in writing the cancelation of the foreign investment record before the 31st of March of the year following the cancellation of the investment.

Can I transfer Foreign Direct Investment capital?

The movement of FDI capital must also be reported to the Central Bank. This procedure is called **substitution**. The substitution and cancellation of foreign investment are considered movements of capital. Whenever there is a change in the titleholders of foreign investment between foreign investors, in the destination or in the company receiving the investment takes place, it is deemed that a substitution occurred. This substitution must be registered by the investor or its representative by submitting a written communication within a maximum period of twelve months after of the substitution.

INTERNATIONAL TREATIES ON FOREIGN INVESTMENT PROTECTION

Overseas Private Investment Corporation - OPIC

Colombia has been covered by the Overseas Private Investment Corporation - OPIC since 1985. OPIC's purpose is to develop U.S.A. investments in developing countries.

It finances and ensures that investment projects contracted with any Colombian State agency are protected against risks such as foreign currency inconvertibility, expropriation and political violence.

Multilateral Investment Guarantee Agency - MIGA

Since 1994, Colombia has been a member of the Multilateral Investment Guaranty Agency (MIGA), a World Bank agency. MIGA is a multilateral agency devoted to guaranteeing foreign investment against non-commercial risks such as foreign currency inconvertibility, discriminatory expropriation and similar measures, contractual default and war and civil riots.

International Center for The Settlement of Investment Disputes – ICSID

The Colombian Congress ratified the creation of the International Center for the Settlement of Investment Disputes (ICSID), covering disputes between states and nationals of other states. ICSID is aimed at protecting foreign investment by offering guaranties and security at the time of solving investment-related disputes.

THE EVOLUTION OF FOREIGN INVESTMENT LEGISLATION IN COLOMBIA

- **Law 45, 1990** - Establishes the government's powers to intervene, inspect, supervise and control the financial markets.
- **Decree 1735, 1993** - Currency exchange purposes, Exchange Operations, Definition of resident in Colombia, Internal Operations)
- **Decree 241, 1999** – Foreign Investment in Colombia
- **Law 963, 2005** - Allows the signing of Legal Stability Contracts (LSCs) between the State and investors for the purpose of stabilizing the rules guiding investment decisions, for up to 20 years.
- **Decree 1940, 2006**
- **Decree 2466, 2007**
- **Decree 1888, 2008**

The foreign exchange regime

- **Decree 2080, 2000** – General Investment Regime
- **Resolution 8, 2000** – issued by the Central Bank
- **Regulatory Circular Letter DCIN 83** – Last update Feb. 10 of 2016.

All the foreign exchange regulations and other legal information is available on the Bank of the Republic website, http://www.banrep.gov.co.

STEP 10: ENJOY YOUR PROPERTY!!

YOU ARE AN OWNER, NOW WHAT?

THE GENERAL OUTLOOK OF THE TAX REGIME IN COLOMBIA

Many foreigners don't buy a house just one time. Some may want to settle down in the country, set up a business, have a real estate portfolio of properties or undertake one of many other commercial activities. This is a general overview of the tax system in Colombia. This page is not advice, but simply the result of my experience and research. Please do not base any decisions upon this -- financial advice is not my professional specialty. If you want solid, professional advice I would suggest that you use the services of experience local legal, accounting and tax firm.

REAL ESTATE TAX

Real estate in Colombia has one tax that encompasses property and land called "Impuesto Predial". It is charged annually and must be paid before the public deed of purchase is granted. You can pay by semesters or for the whole year, which earns you a very good discount. It is estimated as a result of several factors due to "estrato" (area zonification) - the higher the strata, the higher your tax and bills are.

Depending on the land's location, real estate may be also subject to taxes such as "valorización" and "plusvalía".

If there is going to be construction or a modification of the property, there are other contributions that must be paid, including the construction license.

There is no VAT tax for the transfer of real estate.

COLOMBIAN TAXES

The corporate income tax rate is 33%. This rate applies to all Colombian corporations, both SAs (sociedad anónima) and limited liability companies (sociedad limitadas), and all foreign companies including corporations, share-issuing partnerships and foreign branches.

Foreign residents are generally only liable to pay tax on Colombian-sourced income. However, after five years of residence foreign residents will also be taxed on foreign-source income.

Taxable income defined

Colombian companies and entities are subject to income tax on income derived from Colombian and foreign sources. Foreign companies and entities are taxed only on their Colombian-source income.

In general, the following is considered Colombian-source income:

- Profits derived from Colombian companies

- The transfer or exploitation of tangible and intangible goods located within the Colombian territory

- The transfer of goods produced in the country, regardless of the place of transfer

- The rendering of services within the Colombian territory

- The rendering of technical assistance and consulting services, and the execution of turnkey contracts, within or outside Colombia

Foreign-source income generally includes income derived from the transfer or exploitation of tangible or intangible goods located outside Colombia, and income from the performance of services outside the country. Income derived from certain external loans and leasing contracts with foreign entities is not considered domestic-source income.

Taxable income in Colombia is defined as gross income less returns, rebates, discounts, all ordinary costs incurred in obtaining the net income and all allowed deductions. Firms may deduct costs that are necessary and proportionate to the activities performed.

FOREIGN INCOME AND TAX TREATIES

Colombia has double-taxation agreements with Bolivia, Ecuador and Peru in accordance with Andean Community (CAN) provisions. Andean Community members have agreed to avoid double taxation of income and net wealth among themselves, but tax legislation has not been harmonized except for Andean multinational firms (EMA). Profits earned by EMA branches will be taxed only in the country where the branch is located. The portion of dividends distributed by an EMA corresponding to profits earned by a branch in another Andean country will not be taxed in the country of the headquarters. Colombia has also signed tax treaties with Spain and Chile, but their enforceability is subject to conditions.

PERSONAL TAXATION

Colombian nationals and foreign residents in Colombia pay tax on income.

Residency

An individual will be considered a subject of tax for Colombian source income if that person stays in Colombia for more than six months in the tax year, even if the stay is not continuous or if the individual is outside Colombia but that person's family is in Colombia.

Resident individuals are taxed on worldwide income; non-residents are taxed only on Colombian-source income.

After five years residence, income earned outside Colombia also becomes subject to tax.

SPECIAL EXPATRIATE TAX REGIME

According to Colombian law foreign residents are required to pay tax on worldwide income after five years of residency in Colombia, be it continuous or discontinuous. Certain types of income whose source is in Colombia are, however, excluded from this and they must be paid from the first day the foreign citizen is in residence.

After five years of residence, foreign residents will also be taxed on foreign-source income.

PRINCIPAL WAYS OF DOING BUSINESS

The forms of business organization commonly used by foreign investors in Colombia are:

a. Setting up a corporation (joint capital stock corporation -sociedad anónima SA in Spanish, the limited liability company -sociedad limitada-, and simplified stock companies –sociedad por acciones simplificada SAS)

We are going to focus on SAS as it is the one that simplify procedures for setting up a local business and most investors use.

It can be created by private document and is born after registration of its articles of incorporation in the appropriate chamber of commerce, unless the initial contributions include real estate, in which case a public deed is required. The shareholders will respond only up to the limit of their contributions, regardless of the cause of the commitment (taxes, litigations, etc.). The only limitation of the SAS is to trade its securities on the public stock market.

To form a limited liability company the partners (a maximum of 25) must assume liability up to the amount of the respective shares. Capital shares must be fully paid at the time of incorporation but can be reduced later with the permission of the Superintendent of Corporations. Capital may be transferred only by formal assignment. When a capital contribution is made in kind the partners must mutually decide on its value.

The limited liability company differs from the SA principally via the fact that it does not issue shares and the participation of a member-owner is not negotiable on the open market (it is transferable only by formal assignment). The limited liability company is governed by the rules of regular partnerships and is restricted to a maximum of 25 owners; a share corporation may have any number exceeding five.

b. Establishing a branch

Foreign companies that seek to have regular operations in Colombia must establish a branch or subsidiary. Branches or subsidiaries of foreign companies are governed by the Financial Superintendent (for financial entities) or the Superintendent of Corporations (for all others).

The head office must apply to the appropriate Superintendent, stating the type of business the branch will conduct in Colombia, its capital, location, expected duration, possible reasons for termination of business in Colombia and the names of its manager-designate and auditor, who must be Colombian. Proof that the branch's assigned capital has been paid must be provided. A notary public from the chosen domicile of the branch must authenticate a copy of the head office's bylaws and statutes.

Several documents must be presented to the local Chamber of Commerce, including the documents outlining incorporation and the bylaws of the foreign company and the board resolution that authorized the establishment of a branch in Colombia, with details of the capital assigned to the branch and appointment of officers. A statement from the Chamber of Commerce that the books have been registered and a certificate from the managing director and auditor that the capital for the branch has been paid must also be placed on file.

These documents require authentication or notarization by a Colombian consulate and the Ministry of Foreign Affairs in Colombia. Like domestic corporations, branches must submit an annual statement to the Superintendent.

They must pay the same fees, keep the same books and build up the same legal reserves as required of SAs. Once a notary public has authenticated and officially recorded the documents, the same registration steps must be taken as for SAs and limited liability companies.

Replacement of the holder(s) of the investment and any change in the designation of the investment or in the character of the recipient company must be registered with the central bank.

RULES ON URBAN REAL ESTATE, CONSTRUCTION AND RENOVATIONS

URBAN DEVELOPMENT LAW

The urban development law (Law 9 of 1989 and Law 388 of 1997) regulates the use of land by the owners of both urban and rural properties, with the purpose of enforcing the right to own a home and to have access to residential utilities, endeavoring to create and defend the public space, protect the environment and ensure an orderly development of municipalities and districts. Thus, the planning and development of a territory is conceived as a public function where general interests prevail over individual interests, and the rights of private citizens are always respected.

These laws contain the rules that must be followed by cities and towns when planning their territories. In addition to the aforementioned, every city and town must issue a zoning code called a *"Plan de Ordenamiento Territorial"* which describes how the city or town will grow.

Update January 2021: in order to be updated on the continuous and fast development of urban and rural areas in Colombia, and also to stablish housing subsidies as a long-term policy to decrease housing deficit in Colombia, in January 2021, the *Law 2079 of 2021 – Housing and Habitat* was issued. The basic principles stated in this chapter remain the same, however in order to achieve any development it is

important to obtain professional advice to ensure that
you comply with specific regulations.

TERRITORIAL DEVELOPMENT PLANS

The territorial development plans (POTs, for their
Spanish acronym, **Plan de ordenamiento Territorial**)
are documents issued by public municipal and district
administrations setting forth the objectives, guidelines,
policies, strategies, goals, programs, acts and rules
adopted to guide and manage the physical development
and planning of the territory and the use of the land by
the corresponding municipality or district.

Territorial development plans can take one of three
forms depending on the number of inhabitants living in
the municipality or district regulated thereby, as
outlined below:

a) Territorial Development Plans (POTs): These are
prepared and adopted by the authorities of districts and
municipalities with a population of above 100,000
inhabitants.

b) Territorial Development Basic Plans (PBOTs):
These are prepared and adopted by the authorities of
municipalities with a population between 30,000 and
100,000 inhabitants.

c) Territorial Development Outlines (EOTs): These are prepared and adopted by the authorities of municipalities with a population below 30,000 inhabitants.

Each territorial development plan, basic plan or outline has an execution program that defines the actions provided by the development plan and which will be executed during the corresponding municipal or district administration (three years, on average), as set out in the development plan of the corresponding city or district. The execution program includes an activity schedule, the entities responsible for each activity and the resources required.

DURATION OF TERRITORIAL DEVELOPMENT PLANS

The territorial development plans must define the duration of the various activities they contemplate and the conditions that will warrant a revision thereof. Regarding their duration, the law provides between three and six years.

PARTIAL PLANS

These are instruments through which the provisions of the territorial development plans are developed and supplemented based on authorizations arising from general urban development rules established in the

POT, but they only apply to given urban land areas or expansions.

URBAN ZONING PLAN (PLAN ZONAL) AND RURAL ZONING PLAN (PLANES DE ORDENAMIENTO RURAL)

In cities and districts, territorial development plans establish zoning units called "territorial division units" for the purpose of defining the way that the urban land will be planned and used. These units are referenced by different names depending on the development plan of each city or district. The provisions established in the UPZs are lower-rank regulations than the territorial development plans.

The UPZs (which is what urban zoning plans are called in Bogotá) seek to respond to the production dynamics of the city or district and its position in the regional context, involving social actors in the definition of development and control aspects.

In rural areas, the basic planning instrument is the Rural Planning Unit (UPR, in Bogotá). UPRs deal with issues related to natural resources, the management of the city's periphery and the protection of ecological values in a given rural area.

DOCUMENTS AND LICENSES REQUIRED TO BUILD OR REMODEL URBAN REAL ESTATE

The instruments used to develop infrastructure, construction or renovations of real estate property are the Urban Development Licenses, which are authorizations issued by the zoning curators or the municipal or district authority (Planning Office) in charge of authorizing works for urbanization, parceling, division of land into lots, construction, enlargement, adaptation, structural reinforcement, modification, building demolition, lot fencing and public space intervention and occupation within the corresponding district or municipality.

"Planning" (land designing) and "construction" are the main permits/licenses required for carrying out building works. Use of real estate requires a zoning certificate which affirms that the use given to a property is allowed by zoning rules. In addition, for those projects that have a strong impact in cities such as Bogotá, an additional permit called a "Plan de Implantación" must be obtained.

A. Planning license

This license is granted to create public and private spaces and for the construction of utility and road infrastructure works with the purpose of adapting the land for urban construction. These licenses must respect the guidelines set forth by the territorial development plans and any rules that may regulate or develop such plans.

B. Construction license

This type of license, as indicated by its name, is granted for the construction of buildings in urbanized lots according to the regulations set forth by the territorial development plans and any rules that may regulate or develop such plans. Construction licenses can take several forms, among which the most relevant are:

a) *New construction license*: for new construction works on land where no construction has been carried out before

b) *Expansion license*: to increase the construction area of an existing building

c) *Renovation license*: to modify the architectural or structural design of an existing building, without increasing the construction area

d) *Adaptation license*: to change the use of a building or part thereof, guaranteeing that the original building will remain

e) *Restoration license*: to conduct works aimed at partially or fully restoring and adapting a building declared as cultural interest property

f) *Structural reinforcement license*: to intervene or reinforce the structure of one or several buildings

g) *Demolition license*: to fully or partially tear down one of several existing buildings in one or several locations. This license must be issued simultaneously with any other form of construction license.

h) *Fencing license*: to permanently fence or enclose a piece of private property

HOW TO APPLY FOR AN URBAN DEVELOPMENT LICENSE

STEP 1

Prior to requesting an urban development license, the issuer must verify whether the applicant is the lawful owner of the building to be covered thereby.

Urbanization, parceling, subdivision and construction licenses may be requested by the property owners, owners of the property under a trust title and the trustees of such trusts, in which case the license must be applied for by the legal representative of the trust fund. In turn, public space intervention and occupation licenses may be requested by individuals or by the public or private companies intending to occupy such public space.

STEP 2

The following documents must be attached to the urban development license application:

a) A copy of the ownership history and no-lien certificate for the real estate property or properties covered by the application, issued no more than one month prior to the application date by the appropriate public instrument records office.

b) The duly completed sole national license application form.

c) If the applicant is a company, a certificate of existence and legal representation (or equivalent document) issued no more than one month prior to the application date.

d) A duly granted power of attorney, when acting through an attorney.

e) A copy of the document evidencing the payment of the property tax of the past five years for the property or properties to be covered by the license.

f) A drawing indicating the location and identification of the property or properties to be covered by the license.

g) A list of addresses of the properties adjacent to the project under the application.

h) In the case of projects for the construction of low-income housing (V.I.S, or Vivienda de Interés Social), the application must include a written statement indicating under oath that the project will be devoted to such a purpose.

It must be borne in mind that for each type of license, the applicant must submit additional documents such as drawings and technical surveys as required by law.

STEP 3

Once the applicant has defined who the license will be issued to and compiled all the documents to be attached, they must file the application with the urban curator or other appropriate municipal or district authority, as the case may be.

STEP 4

The license application will be numbered consecutively in the chronological order it was received, making a note of the attached documents. Should the application be submitted without all the necessary documents, it will be returned for it to be resubmitted properly.

STEP 5

Once the urban curator or the appropriate municipal or district authority admits the application to study, process and finally issue the license, the immediate neighbors of the property to be licensed are notified to give them an opportunity to become a part of the procedure and exercise their rights.

The notice to the neighbors must indicate: the name of the license applicant, address of the property or properties to be licensed, type of license applied for and proposed use and intensity. This notice must be sent by certified mail. In all cases, third parties may become a part of the administrative procedure and raise objections to the application until the corresponding authority decides to issue or deny the license.

STEP 6

Upon completing the technical and legal review of the application, the urban curator or the competent municipal or district authority will record in minutes the list of remarks on the updates, corrections or clarifications that the applicant must submit with regard to the project. The applicant will have 30 business days, renewable for another 15 business days, to respond to these requirements.

STEP 7

The authority processing the license application must decide whether to issue or deny the license, within no more than 45 business days from the date on which the application is duly and legally filed. Should it fail to respond within the deadline, the license will be understood to have been issued, provided the application submitted does not breach any provisions of the territorial development plan or any rules that may develop or regulate such plan, always supported by certificates issued by the corresponding administrative authorities upon the pertinent notarial procedure (issuance of a public deed invoking the positive administrative silence).

On the contrary, if the authority processing the license application meets the established deadline, it will issue the license through an administrative act. Depending on the magnitude of the project, the deadline to process the application may be extended by up to half the time initially granted, that is, for up to 22 additional business days.

LENGHT OF A LICENSE

The duration of urban development licenses is limited depending on their type.

Therefore, urbanizing, parceling and construction licenses may be effective over 24 months and renewable for 12 additional months, but if the urbanizing and construction licenses are applied for simultaneously, their duration will be 36 months, renewable for an additional 12-month period. These duration conditions are not applicable to licenses for urban development projects that are to be performed in stages, since these projects are subject to a special legal treatment (24 months for the authorized stage).

COST AND TIME INVOLVED IN OBTAINING A LICENSE

The appropriate cost of a permit depends on the cost of the building. The formulas to calculate the expenses are indicated in article 107 of Decree 564, issued in 2006. In normal circumstances a building permit can be obtained in about 45 working days (except for a "*Plan de Implantación*" which takes much longer).

If the competent authority does not issue the license, request additional information or reject the petition, an implied authorization shall be deemed granted by means of a "Positive Governmental Silence", which means that the petitioner will be deemed to be covered by a license as long as the construction fulfill all urban regulations.

However, neighbors and the community may exert opposition rights, and this can cause delays.

URBAN DEVELOPMENT AUTHORITIES

Zoning curators

Zoning curators (*Curadores Urbanos*) are private individuals commissioned to perform a public function and are in charge of studying, processing and issuing urban development licenses.

They are appointed by the city or district mayor through a merit-based selection process and their commission is valid for five years, renewable if the administrative authority deems it advisable.

Zoning curators work in coordination with the Ministry of Environment, Housing and Territorial Development and with City Hall and the corresponding planning offices. In turn, these two authorities supervise and control the curators.

Public Instrument Records Office

This is the office in charge of keeping a real estate property record in a given district or municipality by recording the various inscriptions or cancellations that are entered on the real estate registration sheet of each property. Documents that may be inscribed or cancelled in the real estate registration record include acts, contracts and court orders that modify or restrict the right of possession or any other right affecting any piece of real estate.

Ministry of Environment, Housing and Territorial Development

Through its Territorial Development Director, the Ministry of Environment, Housing and Territorial Development handles all issues pertaining to urban and territorial development rules.

The Ministry is responsible for coordinating and following up on urban curators, with the purpose of guiding and supporting their adequate implementation within local administrations. The Ministry may recommend to municipal or district mayors the creation and designation of new urban curator's offices.

City Halls

Through their planning office or the office acting in its stead, city and district mayors are responsible for coordinating the timely formulation of the territorial development plan and submitting it to the consideration of the City Council.

Additionally, Mayors supervise and control zoning curators to ensure their compliance with applicable rules and constitute a second instance in the case of lawsuits filed by private parties against the government. Furthermore, the mayor's office is responsible for the ex-post control of works authorized by the appropriate authorities or of those built without a corresponding license.

The mayor or his delegate may impose sanctions in the event that a private party infringes upon an urban development rule. These sanctions include ordering that the works be modified to adapt to the licenses and current regulations, imposing fines, sealing off the works and/or demolishing the work already done without a license or in violation of the license provisions.

The Geographic Institute Agustin Codazzi

The Geographic Institute Agustín Codazzi (IGAC for its Spanish acronym) is the Government entity responsible for producing the official maps and basic cartography of Colombia and managing the national cadastral infrastructure and the national soil survey. IGAC also distributes geographic data in the form of its online portal, SIGOT.

USE OF RURAL SUBURBAN LAND

a. Conditions for the use of commercial and services land

The granting of parceling and construction licenses for the development of commercial and services projects with a construction area of more than five thousand square meters on rural suburban land is only allowed in areas specifically earmarked in the maps contained in the territorial development plans or in the rural planning units.

Occupation indexes may not exceed 30% of the total area and the rest will be devoted preferably to the preservation or restoration of native vegetation.

b. Conditions for the use of industrial land

The territorial development plan or the rural planning units must contemplate at least the cartographical delineation of industrial activity areas in rural suburban lands, maximum heights and volumetric rules applicable to the development of industrial uses, in order to protect the rural landscape. Urban development rules must also contemplate the lateral and back space to be left with regard to adjacent properties. The areas for operation of cargo vehicles and the parking spaces required for the correct application of the corresponding use, including loading and unloading operations, must be built inside the properties constituting the minimum performance unit or the industrial park, grouping or complex.

Occupation indexes may not exceed 30% of the total property area in the case of a minimum performance unit or 50% in the case of industrial parks, groupings or complexes. The rest will be devoted, preferably, to the preservation or restoration of native vegetation. Without prejudice to the obligation to comply with all the other rules stipulated in this decree, the maximum width of suburban "road corridors" devoted exclusively to industrial purposes will be 500 meters measured from the edge of the road. In no case may the area of industrial parks, groupings or complexes fall below ten hectares.

USE OF RURAL NON-SUBURBAN LAND FOR INDUSTRIAL ACTIVITIES

The current area used by the industrial activity or other areas devoted to similar purposes may not be extended, regardless of the name they take in rural non-suburban land. Nor can new areas be created, except in the case of areas devoted to natural resource exploitation or development of agribusiness, ecotourism, agro tourism, aqua tourism or other similar activities compatible with the agricultural, cattle-raising or forest vocation of rural lands.

Occupation indexes may not exceed 30% of the total area and the rest will be devoted preferably to the preservation or restoration of native vegetation.

The location of rural industrial use land sites requires a classification that takes into account the environmental and landscape impact produced, and which establishes its compatibility with regard to all other uses allowed in rural lands. Until such classification is included in the territorial development plans or in the rural planning units, license applications for the development of industrial uses in rural lands will be subject to the favorable opinion of the Regional Environmental Authority (Corporación Autónoma Regional) or the Sustainable Development Authority, regarding the way the project will affect the renewable natural resources and the environment, in addition to any additional licenses, permits and other environmental authorizations applicable to each individual case.

RENTING REAL ESTATE IN COLOMBIA

THINGS TO BEAR IN MIND WHEN RENTING REAL ESTATE

Colombian law is guided by two constitutional principles: (i) the property must comply with a social purpose, and (ii) every person has the right to a proper dwelling.

For years the lease of a property was a headache for homeowners, since the law favored the tenant. This law has recently moved in the direction of achieving a balance between the rights of landlords and tenants. Landlords and real estate brokers have an organized lobby force in Congress and have been very successful in recent years in obtaining stronger protection from the law. To encourage investment in property and protect the assets of the owners of properties, the government issued Law 820 in 2003, which is summarized below:

LEASES

A lease contract can be undertaken in verbal or written form, and rent can be set freely by agreement between the landlord and tenant and must include at least:

- Name and identification of all parties.

- Identification of the property.

- The area that is leased, and service areas shared with other occupants.

The contract should specify the price and form of payment and the length of term and appointment of the party who are responsible for payment of utilities.

The contract is understood to be extended if the parties have complied with the obligations.

For each year of the lease the landlord may increase the fee up to a ratio not exceeding 100% of the increase incurred by the consumer price index (CPI) of the previous year. The monthly price cannot exceed one percent of the market value of the property or the part that is being given to lease.

The commercial value cannot exceed two times the cadastral value of the dwelling at the time of the contract.
If the owner insists on a larger increase, the tenant can sue.

TERMINATION OF CONTRACT

The parties at any time and in consensus can terminate the contract.

Provisions applying to termination of the contract by the landlord

- If the tenant is not complying with their obligations, e.g., if they default on rent payments or public utilities payments.

- If the tenant is not in default, the landlord can terminate the contract during the renewal terms (not during the initial term) by sending written notice of termination to the tenant three months prior to the effective date of termination, informing them that the indemnification ordered by law will be paid. Such indemnification, equivalent to three months of rent, has to be deposited with the entities authorized by the government, who will then forward it to the tenant.

- Likewise, the landlord can terminate the contract at the end of the initial term or of any of the renewal terms by sending written notice to the tenant three months prior to the date of termination of the contract, if: (i) the landlord will need the dwelling for their own habitation for not less than 1 year; (ii) the dwelling has to be demolished to undertake new construction; (iii) the dwelling has to be emptied to be repaired; or (iv) the dwelling has been sold and it has to be passed to the buyer (in this case the landlord does not have to indemnify the tenant so long as he complies with the three month notice period).

- The landlord can also terminate the contract if it has lasted no less than four years, by paying an indemnification equivalent to 1.5 months of rent.

Provisions applying to termination of the contract by the tenant

- The tenant can unilaterally terminate the contract at any time if the landlord breaches their contractual and legal duties, e.g., when they interferes with the quiet enjoyment of the dwelling by the tenant.

- The tenant can also unilaterally terminate the contract during the initial term or any of the renewal terms by sending written notice of termination to the landlord three months prior to the effective date of termination, informing them that the indemnification ordered by law will be paid. Such indemnification, equivalent to three months of rent, has to be deposited with the entities authorized by the government, which will then forward it to the landlord.

- Finally, the tenant can terminate the contract at the end of the initial term or of any of the renewal terms by sending written notice to the landlord three months prior to the date of termination of the contract. No indemnification is required in this case.

In the absence of written evidence of notice, the lease shall be deemed automatically renewed for a term equal to that initially agreed.

The most important change in the new law is that it strengthens the legal tools so that in the case of a default by the tenant, the property can be recovered no later than six months after the default.

Prior to the issuance of the law, this process could take up to ten years, but the mechanisms have now been given to the owner to protect their wealth. In addition, if required the tenant will be responsible for paying court costs and any fees that might arise as a result of their default or breach of contract.

PUBLIC UTILITIES

When payment of utilities is the responsibility of the tenant, the landlord may require the provision of guarantees or collateral to guarantee the payment of invoices to the companies providing the services.

If payment is not undertaken, the responsibility lies with the tenant and utility companies may take those actions as may be held against the tenant.

DOCUMENTS NEEDED TO COMPLETE A LEASE TRANSACTION

To rent a property an individual must show proof of their ability to pay the base rent. Depending on whether it is a real estate company or a private owner, they may be required to present any or all of the following documents to prove their ability to pay:

For individuals:

- Proof of income equivalent to three times the value of the rent.

- A copy of their most recent tax statement.

- A copy of their most recent company's payroll receipt which must include salary, position and the time worked for the same company.

- Two fiadores: a person (or an entity) who owns property in Colombia and who can act as a guarantor. The fiador must also show proof of ownership and proof of no encumbrances of their ownership.

- Payment in advance of at least six months of the base rent.

For companies:

- An executed lease between the landlord and tenant.

- A copy of the company's legal constitution.

- A copy of the authorization indicating the representative for signing documents.

- A copy of the company's audited financial statements.

- A copy of their most recent tax statement.

- If the company is new, they must provide full documentation for its partners, outlining their income and payment capacities.

- 2 fiadores: a person (or an entity) who owns property in Colombia and who can act as a guarantor. The fiador must also show proof of ownership and proof of no encumbrances of their ownership.

FAQ FOR LEASING IN COLOMBIA

What measures under the law protect the owner in case of default by the lessee?

In the case of delay in payment of rent and utilities the Act. 820 of 2003 (*Ley de Arriendos*), provides protective measures including the seizure of the tenant's assets.

The eviction process can be initiated at 30 days past due, without judicial process.

How can you guarantee payment of public services?

The landlord must inform the utility companies that the property is leased so that they in turn convey the required guarantees to the new tenant.

The landlord may also seek a guarantee or bond from the landlord and notify the utility companies who is inhabiting the building. If the owner does not report or have the required insurance policy, the account will be on their charge.

How should I calculate the rental fee?

Usually, a rental fee is based on the market price of the area. However, you need to bear in mind that monthly fees may not exceed one percent of the market value of the property.

What is the landlord bound by?

Landlords are required to deliver the property in good condition at the time of the signing of the contract and to keep utilities in the property in good condition. In the case of condominium properties, they must give the tenant a copy of the relevant rules.

What is the tenant bound by?

The tenant must pay the price of the lease within the stipulated time, take care of the property and things received via rent, pay services on time and comply with the condo rules, where appropriate.

What does the rent specifically include and what additional charges is the tenant responsible for?

- Base rent to the landlord.

- IVA (Value Added Tax) for all fees.

- Maintenance fees are quoted separately and they are considered additional to the base rent. This includes common areas such as a lobby, staircases, reception areas and parking.

- Leasing Insurance (3.5%) will cover leasing expenses in case of early cancellation or legal trial (including electricity, phone, water, etc.).

- 50% Impuesto Timbre (when the total value of the contract surpasses 80 million Colombian pesos this tax is mandatory and the rate is 1.50 pesos for each 1,000 pesos of the total value of the contract).

- Electricity, water and gas expenses (independently measured).

- Telephone expenses.

What charges is the landlord responsible for?

- Realty taxes.

- Extraordinary administration expenses.

- Brokerage commissions are equal to one or two months rent depending on the lease extension and they apply in cases where there is no management involved in the lease.

- When a property management company is managing the rent, the real estate commission is paid monthly and it can vary between eight to ten percent of the base rent (this value is deducted monthly from the base rent).

What units is rent quoted in?

The rent can be fixed in any currency, but if fixed in a foreign currency it has to be paid in Colombian pesos at the market exchange rate that is in force at the time of the contract, unless otherwise agreed by the parties. Rents are quoted in Colombian Pesos per square meter per month. There are 10.76 square feet in one square meter.

How is rent paid?

The rent is paid on a monthly basis within the first five days of the period, usually in advance at the landlord's address. Alternatively, the landlord may hire a manager to collect the rent in their name.

CONCLUSION

Congratulations! You are now the happy owner of a property in Colombia.

During this journey that we have been together through this book, we've covered all the process of buying and investing in Colombia real estate, and now you have the full context for these secrets.

Remember, this is a guide. Don't just read it once and go on with business as usual. Keep it handy. You can consult any step that you are in, and refer to it often according to your needs.

You now have all the knowledge to accomplish your real estate dreams, and I want you to quickly re-walk you through the entire real estate process:

Step # 1. Choose the location. Get enough information about your favorite Colombian city.

Step # 2. Choose the property. New, used, apartment, house, off-plan projects, commercial, for rent, to own, vacation home.

Step # 3. Make an offer and negotiate the price the Colombian way .

Step # 4. Define your payment method, so you can take the best out of your money.

Step # 5. Sign a purchase agreement and have all in written.

Step # 6. Make the closing and sign the deed.

Step # 7. Prepare to receive your property, no matter whether you can or can't come to Colombia.

Step # 8. Register the ownership of the property, to secure your rights.

Step # 9. Register your property as a foreign investment.

Step # 10. Enjoy your property!

This is the game. I hope that you can use these information to get your dream property, and be secure about your hard earned money.

Thank you for allowing me serving you through these pages, and it's very fulfillment to know that this words can do as much for you as you are going to a new journey in this beautiful country that I love as much as you surely do too.

I hope you can hit me in any of the social media platforms, to say hi, and please share if this information was useful or not, and let me know everything you think that can be improved.

See you in Colombia!

Thanks,

Mauricio Jaimes

P.S. Don't forget: It's not the information you can get, It's about how to use it…

ABOUT THE AUTHOR

My name is Mauricio Jaimes, I'm a generation X guy born in Bucaramanga, Santander Province, Colombia. I'm married and I have three beautiful kids, which are the driving force of my life.

I'm an **Industrial Engineer**. I got my degree from the Javeriana University in Bogotá in 1994, where I lived for 6 years. During this time, I started my first foray as property investor while looking for the right apartment where I would spend my college years.

My first working experience was at Las Villas Aval Group, a banking firm specializing in housing lends. When I was done with this career I returned to my hometown to work in the family business. My father had been in the real estate and construction business for more than 40 years, so I had the privilege to have a great mentor in the field. The company is called **Urviviendas** and it focuses on developing middle class housing projects, real estate, property investment and public works projects. I have spent the **last 25 years of my professional experience** at my family company, working in all phases of real estate development. I have been Director of Construction, Project Manager, Operations Manager, and Sales Manager. I also have been involved in the creation of each homeowners association and the governing documents for every project we have developed. Currently I serve as an advisory Board Member.

I also partnered with one of the most important firms in Colombia as a real estate agent, specializing in offering international real estate investment in the **US and Panama** to Colombian investors.

Married and with two little babies, in 2000 I went to **France** to get a Master's degree in **International Business** from the Grenoble Graduate School of Business in Grenoble, France. It was a wonderful experience, not only for me but for all the family, including the kids.

The best aspect of this was the friendships I made with people in different parts of the world and the way it made me have a more open mind with different cultures.

I also know what it feels like to be a foreign person trying to find an **apartment** for a family, as I was not fluent in French and had to have an appendix removal surgery three days after arriving!

I've always been fascinated with the **internet's** capacity to be a powerful business tool, so I did my degree's dissertation project on **e-procurement**.

Throughout my experience in the **real estate and construction** business, I've been in contact with a lot of Colombian people who live abroad and have bought property mostly for relatives and so on. Some of them are married to foreigners and I have helped them with their major concern: how to **buy safety** in Colombia as a foreign investor.

In 2007, when I was making a deal with a foreigner in one of our developments, I noticed that there was not much online information in English about the buying process in **Colombia**. And even though it is not rocket science, for people abroad who are visiting the country for the first time, it becomes increasingly difficult when they don't know the language, laws, local customs, neighborhoods, etc.

That's why I created this guide, to provide **non-Spanish speakers** the most accurate information about how to buy real estate in Colombia and to help them throughout the process by offering my consultant services and experience in the real estate business.

My site ranks on the first page in Google for the keywords "**Colombia real estate**", among millions of sites. We are a matchmaker for buyers who look for information about the Colombian market and sellers who want to offer their Colombian properties to the international market. I also offer my consultant services in real estate and property investment.

ABOUT BUYCOLOMBIAREALTY.COM

BuyColombiaRealty.com is a website that specializes in marketing and promoting real estate in Colombia to international markets.

I can say for sure we were pioneers as the first real estate company focused on the international customer interested in Colombian real estate. Our website has been the leader in the promotion and marketing of real estate in Colombia for the foreign market and we have had success on the Internet as the website with the most exposure on search engines in this category.

Our goal is to become the first real estate source of information in Colombia for the international market.

We offer:

To potential international and local buyers: Advisory services for the process of buying or investing in real estate in Colombia, via clear, comprehensive and quality information on the range of real estate in Colombia and related services.

To developers, agents and brokers: A channel for marketing projects through marketing tools and online customer tracking to expand to the overseas market and therefore increase project sales.

THE KEY TO SUCCESS WITH OUR MARKETING SERVICES:

a. Our online Traffic

Having a website is not enough. You need a website that has traffic... and more importantly, traffic that targets your niche market!

This is where we make a difference. BuyColombiaRealty.com is has become well positioned in all major search engines without paying a single dollar in ad campaigns.

Thanks to our site content, BCR has ranked among the most visited sites, and holds the first position in major search engines for the most common terms used by foreigners and investors interested in real estate in Colombia. (e.g., you can type the term "Colombia real estate" in Google and see our leadership listed over millions of other internet sites.)

On average we register 20,000 monthly visits from real people worldwide who have found valuable and important information on our site when searching for information on real estate in Colombia.

b. Our International Exposure

Thanks to our traffic and our content, we have been reviewed by leading international media and web portals which generates broad national and international exposure for our partners and clients. Among the most significant reviews are:

New York Times "Great Homes and Destinations"

Colombia For Sale in...

http://www.nytimes.com/2009/03/11/greathomesanddestinations/11gh-sale-1.html?_r=1

New York Times - Colombia's capital Find new sense of optimism

http://www.nytimes.com/2010/01/29/greathomesanddestinations/29iht-rebogota.html?ref=global-home

W radio in Colombia, a member of the European media group Prisa Interview (In Spanish).

http://www.wradio.com.co/oir.aspx?id=777545

Expatexchange.com, one of the main places for retirees on the internet, published articles

http://www.expatexchange.com/lib_rd.cfm?articleid=2876&networkid=32

International Living Magazine, published, with 452,000 online subscribers and 52,000 subscribers to its printed edition.

http://www.buycolombiarealty.com/support-files/il_july_issue.pdf

The Colombian market offers endless opportunity, and we have the tools to exploit it.

Visit our website at www.buycolombiarealty.com

CPSIA information can be obtained
at www.ICGtesting.com
Printed in the USA
LVHW060232280222
712185LV00009B/407